# PORTRAITS IN RHYME

$2⁻   3\97

Dedicated to my sister,
Judith Anne Albert-McKinney,
woman of courage and compassion.

# ABOUT THE AUTHOR

Brother John Albert was born in Jersey City, New Jersey, on February 20, 1948. He completed his primary education at Roman Catholic schools in New Jersey and Indiana. He studied at the Latin School of Indianapolis and Saint Mary's Seminary in Kentucky. He holds the Bachelor of Arts degree in Philosophy and the Master of Divinity degree from Saint Meinrad Seminary in Indiana. John was ordained Cleric, Porter and Lector in 1971, and Acolyte in 1972, for the Archdiocese of Indianapolis. He entered Holy Spirit Abbey, Conyers, Georgia, on June 29, 1974, and professed his Solemn Vows as a monk of the Order of the Cistercians of the Strict Observance (Trappists) on July 16, 1983. He has held membership in The American Benedictine Academy, The International Thomas Merton Society, and The Conyers/Rockdale Council for the Arts. He founded The Honey Creek Poets Society in 1992. In 1994, in celebration of Holy Spirit Abbey's Golden Jubilee of Foundation, he co-curated monastic exhibits at Oxford College of Emory University; Georgia College in Milledgeville; and The Gallery of the Conyers/Rockdale Council for the Arts. He publishes and lectures on spiritual themes and such literary figures as Henry David Thoreau, Thomas Merton and Flannery O'Conner. He is currently at work on a study of D. H. Lawrence and human intimacy.

Brother John Albert, OCSO, M.Div.

# PORTRAITS IN RHYME
## Poems and Poems in Prose 1965-1996

Foreword by Patricia A. Schwab
Introduction by Sue Loman

Verba Ad Verbum

MONASTIC IMPRESSIONS 1996

Typeset by Sue Loman. Pre-press work by Accu-Print, Inc., Conyers, Georgia. Printed by Advanced Data Reproductions, Inc., Wichita, Kansas.


First Edition: First Impression
November 1996
1000 Copies
Library of Congress Catalog Card Number: 96-79615
ISBN: 0-9655524-0-3
Published with the permission of the Superior


Please address all correspondence to:

Brother John Albert, OCSO, M.Div.
Holy Spirit Abbey
2625 Highway 212, SW
Conyers, Georgia 30208-4044

# A NOTE ON THE TEXT

PORTRAITS IN RHYME: POEMS AND POEMS IN PROSE 1965-1996 is a comprehensive collection of verse by Brother John Albert, OCSO, arranged in chronological order by date of composition. This collection reprints all the poems contained in JOHN ALBERT*POEMS 1965-1992 (John Otto Schwab, Publisher 1993) and JOHN ALBERT*POEMS II 1965-1994 (John Otto Schwab, Publisher 1994), as well as edited versions of all the poems in NO CAUSE FOR SHAME: POEMS ABOUT MEN BY ONE OF THEM (The Honey Creek Poets Society 1995). Please consult these volumes for introductory material; annotations on date and place of composition; first publication references; acknowledgements for sources quoted; and original dedications. A small number of poems have been retitled to express content rather than geographical location. The earlier texts have been corrected and amended where necessary. Thirty-two new poems are published here for the first time; a few of them are fragments which were later worked into longer compositions. In this way, we can watch the evolution of the author and his writings. Our text represents thirty years of reflection and composition and four years of collecting and editing autograph manuscripts, original typescripts, revisions, drafts and photocopies. In 1992, with the help of Anthony Todd Pollard, first President of The Honey Creek Poets Society, we assembled all the original manuscripts and typescripts into three volumes: I. THE PRE-MONASTIC POEMS 1962-1973; II. THE MONASTERY POEMS 1974-1992; III. THE RE-EDUCATION OF A TIMID MONK 1974-1989. This initial sorting, selecting and editing process was completed on April 8, 1992. A fourth volume, listing the poems in chronological order, was then drawn up. These four volumes became the *typica* or foundational document for all the publishing of Brother John's poetical work to the present, with compositions being added as the author continued to work. Reverend Father, Dom Bernard Johnson, OCSO, Brother John's Abbot, has been instrumental in this project from the start, granting his permission for publication at each stage and being most helpful in the actual hands-on work with written texts in all their nuances. Dom Bernard's literary and religious sensibilities and his pastoral care for the author are readily acknowledged. We are grateful to him. From July of 1995 to October of 1996, our text, initially under the title A RECORD OF MY PASSING, has gone through fourteen drafts and eight typescripts. It can be pointed out that the author is also a widely published essayist. A selection of his early theological reflections (1966-1973) was published by The Honey Creek Poets Society in 1995. A 1973 study, "Religious Symbolism and Dream Interpretation," was also published by The Honey Creek Poets Society during that year. Other early investigations--oriental essays on Buddhist Ethics and Hindu and Gnostic spirituality; a patristic study on original sin in the theology of the early Fathers of the Church--await publication. The poems in PORTRAITS IN RHYME were being written while Brother John was publishing papers on William Shakespeare, John Keats, Henry David Thoreau, Oscar Wilde, Cardinal Newman, Dietrich Bonhoeffer, Bob Dylan, Thomas Merton and Saint

Augustine of Hippo, as well as many diverse spiritual, biblical and monastic themes. Since 1993 Brother John has been bringing his experience and insights to a larger audience through lecturing and group meditation sessions. New poems, not collected here, will be assembled in a companion volume sometime in the future. We hope PORTRAITS IN RHYME will remain a definitive text for your enjoyment and growth. It is a mature book by a mature monk intended for those who are serious about their emotional and spiritual development.

# A NOTE ON THE ILLUSTRATIONS

# TABLE OF CONTENTS

# FOREWORD

We are the author of our own lives. The hardest thing is to look into our own soul. To look at who we are. We're each on our own path: childhood, past experience, time and place. Our truth, our beauty, is given as a gift, and what we do with this gift determines who we are and who we become. Sometimes life does not allow us a lot of options and choices. Sometimes it is "comfortable" not to have choices. Sometimes we go through life with fears of abandonment without knowing it. We must each face our own fears. No one can do it for us. In some families men are never allowed to express emotion, especially anger. Men may do it publicly in politics and war and business but remain repressed personally. A boy is sometimes told: *"Grow up!" "Snap out of it!"* This causes problems later in life. All of Brother John Albert's writings are integrated with his personhood. While some of John's characters and situations might be fictional, his poems are not fiction. He tells it "like it is!" He doesn't "flower it up." The "stuff" of the troubles is still there in the present. John's faced his fears. He's come through. He's done it. He can be proud of himself. John has courage. He has strength. Life, in the monastery, in marriage, in any human circumstance, is not "black or white." Choices are made, vows are made, but we continue to grow and change. We never say: *"This is it!"* Or: *"If you're not happy, leave!"* We can go through changes in minutes. Sometimes I've wondered if John is in the right place. There are so many limits to his creativity, so many constraints on his intellectual energies. As he will admit, John never experienced the ordinary "rites of passage" for a young man in our society. But I've come to see that it was I who could not at first understand John's solitary nature and that the monastery is more than a "haven of security" for him. John is a fighter. He is tough. He is a monk. There is reverence in John's rebellion. He is not phony in his religion. Every writer has the right to write whatever he wants. There is no such thing as a "good" or "bad" poem. When written with a sincere heart and a pure intention, a poem is a single, unique revelation, of a single, unique person. Just as the person, the poem is. John is not a "player." There is an emotional honesty in his writing, even when "his" ideal and reality may not seem to match "ours." John gives us permission to enter into his own emotional space. He is not giving us food for gossip. He is not playing jeopardy with his reputation. He knows who he is and is secure in his self-knowledge. He is not intentionally being dangerous. He is writing good things with good intentions, risking the possibility of bad interpretations for the sake of the poet's truth: the truth of himself and our truth as his readers. John has a freedom of feelings and expressions which cannot be taken away. I would never dream of taking it away from him by censoring him or being judgmental of him. In the editing process, I asked John: *"Is this really* *you*?" I have only reminded him of his responsibilities and cautioned him about the cruelty of others, usually those afraid of their own truth. John's truth can be ominous. John has a faith so profound as to go down deeper into that realm of the spirit where realities are realities, without need of symbolization. Pain is pain, no matter how John puts it into words. I think I know the "real" John and John has helped me come to discover and embrace the "real" me. I love the simple spirituality in John, the spontaneity and balance and directness I desire in my own life. His actual talk is great and you hear it in the simpler, shorter poems, the "down to earth" poems, the poems about us ordinary, common people. John has come to see things in right perspective and right proportion. This book is full of intensity and is at times terribly intellectual. I think this happens when John tends to make things too high brow and complicated, such as he does in some of his early writings--perhaps to speak to those in scholarly situations. But this is my point. Through his writings, we meet so many of John's friends in their actual life situations. I've come to love them because John took time to tell us about them, to hold them up to us in his compassion for them. There will always be those who will look for something flawed in John and something negative in his writings. But I know John got here before they did and came through all the greater for his self-scrutiny. There is now a "Father Wisdom" and a "Mother Wisdom" in his spirit, and in his writings. The change in him, even since the publication of JOHN ALBERT*POEMS in 1993, has been remarkable: I sense it, I see it, I hear it in his voice. PORTRAITS IN RHYME gives me hope for my own continued transformation and guiding words along my way.

Patricia A. Schwab, President Emeritus
The Honey Creek Poets Society
52 Grove Street
Bergenfield, New Jersey 07621

# INTRODUCTION

I would like to begin my introduction by repeating what I wrote in my first letter as President of the Honey Creek Poets Society. Approximately two years ago, September 1993, when I spoke to Brother John Albert for the first time, he asked me to break the law! Yes, this timid, mild-mannered, soft-spoken monk did that. (Well, that is how I thought of monks—at least at that time.) He called the school where I am employed and asked for the address of a former graduate, Mr. Tim Willis. Tim, who had been blind since ten years of age, had inspired Brother John to write a poem, THE GENTLE DECEPTION. Brother John wished to send Tim a copy of the poem. Schools are not allowed to give out this information. I did drop some hints which did not prove to be helpful at all. John called back several weeks later and asked for my help again. How could I not provide it? I called Tim's home, spoke with his mother and she gave me permission to give Brother John any information at all that he might need. After more than a year of correspondence and telephone conversations, Brother John and Tim finally met at the school on December 28, 1994. His poem, THE GENTLE DECEPTION, will indicate to you Brother John's deep respect for Tim as a world class runner and gold medalist athlete. Shortly after Brother John's first call asking me for help, he sent me a thank-you note. About this time I offered to help him with his work as a poet and essayist after reading a number of his works which he had mailed to me. As a typesetter, I realized that writers always needed help in getting their work into print. At first I thought if I ever had a working relationship with Brother John it would consist of phone calls and the postal service. I did not dream that I would ever meet him. Many months later, I received a written invitation to The Garden of Contemplation Exhibit in honor of Holy Spirit Abbey's Golden Jubilee of Foundation, a 50th anniversary retrospective sponsored by the Conyers/Rockdale Council for the Arts and co-curated by Brother John. Then, on November 8, 1994, the date of the open house for the exhibit, Brother John, this gentle, gentle monk, called and asked if I had received the invitation and would I attend. I did not plan to attend. Now, what was I to do? How could I *not* attend? And so it came to pass—I met Brother John! My remembrance of the first time I met Brother John is of a short, white-haired man, very soft-spoken, with a typical monk's haircut and wearing a typical monk's habit. Surprisingly, I never considered his age. At my first meeting with Brother John at the monastery, I was a nervous wreck. He seemed so sure of himself and spoke so freely to me. He had tons and tons of paper work with him and gave me more information than I could comprehend. I could not believe he had kept almost everything he had ever written. I regret not having the opportunity to read those early writings now lost to us. When he learned of the death of his boyhood hero in Texas on August 13, 1995, John told me about SEVEN SHADES OF GREEN, a poem written after seeing Mickey Mantle play in Yankee Stadium. And I wish we still had SHE'S GOT THE SWEETEST LITTLE TULIPS, a ditty about one of his grade school girlfriends. I think she shows up in MY CONFIDANTÉ. John spoke on and on about being a monk and a writer and what he hoped to accomplish. I didn't know what to say, so I asked, "*Are you famous?*" I was serious and he did not laugh. I thought perhaps I had offended him. His actual response was, "*I am well known in certain circles.*" By this point, John had already been published in MONASTIC EXCHANGE, THE MERTON SEASONAL, THE MERTON ANNUAL, THE GEORGIA BULLETIN, LUTHERAN FORUM, THE ROCKDALE CITIZEN, CISTERCIAN STUDIES, THE AMERICAN BENEDICTINE REVIEW and other journals and periodicals. His study, "The Christ of Oscar Wilde," had been anthologized by Macmillan and Company.

## TYPESETTING AND LITERARY ASSISTANCE

John told me he felt confident that God had sent me into his life to help preserve and publish his works. He asked me to be his typesetter and literary assistant, a relationship which would allow us to be friends and co-workers. I had been thinking about "doing something to help somebody" and here was my opportunity. By December, 1994, I had already typeset my first manuscript for John, "The Incursion of the Word: Learning to Hear, Read and Write Again the Monastic Way," a study prepared for the journal, WORD & SPIRIT, consisting of a text of 40,000 words and a bibliography of 18,000 words. Shortly into 1995, John asked me to serve as the Fourth President of the Honey Creek Poets Society, a literary association founded by him in 1992. Our second effort was organizing files of everything that had been published from the start to the present. My typeset list was printed in booklet form under the title of JOHN ALBERT, OCSO, M.DIV., BIBLIOGRAPHY OF PUBLISHED WORKS: 1968-1994 (Honey Creek Poets Society, February 1995). Next, I typeset a series of personal and liturgical prayers, published as PRAYERS: 1972-1984 (Honey Creek Poets Society, April 1995). Our fourth project was a selection of essays composed at Saint Mary's Seminary in Kentucky and at Saint Meinrad Seminary, EARLY ESSAYS: 1966-1973 (Honey Creek Poets Society, June 1995). Once again John's discipline was impressive and range of interest extraordinary. We hear about Cicero on love, Solon on ethics, Pope Paul VI on liturgy, David Knowles on medieval thought, Meister Eckhart on mysticism, John of the Cross, and (Lord, help the typesetter) Saint Athanasius on the life of Saint Antony. Working with John is like working with no one I have ever known. His mind works like no other. He is in a class all his own and works in a way all his own. I could sit for hours and listen to him talk about things that fascinate him, but what? Everything! Everything fascinates John. Witness the diversity of his poems. He is truly brilliant and perhaps this is the basis for his struggle with himself, the rest of us mortals and life in general.

## A PERSON AND WRITER OF EXTREME SENSITIVITY

I would like to say more about my early visits with Brother John Albert at the monastery. Before I met John, I truly believed that monks had no feelings except extreme love for the universe. Surely they did not know anger, hatred, jealousy, desire, etc. I assumed sometime during their schooling something just enveloped them and took away all worldly feelings. I truly believed, now that I think of it, monks were like eunuchs from an old biblical movie. Could there be anyone more *naivé* about monks? Now it's hard to believe how *naivé* I was. At our second meeting, Brother John spoke as if he were lost. He did not seem to like or love himself. I wondered: *"If John does not love himself, how can he live with and love his brother monks?"* I listened in total surprise not knowing what to say. I knew whatever I said would be inadequate; then I realized that John did not expect a response. He only wanted me to listen to him. I did not see strength. What I saw I thought was despair. John seemed to be at a low point in his life. Later on, when Brother John was waiting to meet Tim Willis, he said, *"I am so nervous."* This took me totally by surprise. I could not imagine how anyone who had accomplished what John had and lived the life that John lived would be nervous about meeting anyone. In my mind, I assumed he knew "everyone" and that one more person could not possibly make him nervous. Again, I was quite *naivé*. Monks are just like the rest of us mortals, and John would want to be the first to say it. John's nervousness in meeting Tim was the shyness of anyone meeting someone new. John's nervousness was another mark of his respect, his sense of awe and honor in the presence of someone he holds in high regard. And, as you can image, the blind gold medalist and the shy monk twice his age got along just fine and continue as good friends today. I think John in someway finds himself in every younger person he admires and in someway lives "unlived" parts of his life through them. Our friendship involves discussions from my perspective as a woman from Middle Tennessee, a divorcee, mother of one daughter and grandmother of two granddaughters. John seeks out people who are very much unlike him so he might learn from them and perhaps give something in return. I try to explain how life is on the "outside." John wants to hear the truth about himself and his life from me as I see it. Sometimes the truth can be painful. Regardless of what I have to say, John will listen. I'm not always sure what he thinks about it at times, but he does listen. Sometimes it seems Brother John is out of touch with contemporary society: the pressure of a 9 to 5 job; the expense of living in society; the almost impossible task of keeping a set schedule; marriage not being the ideologically romantic existence he desires for everyone he cares about; the world being full of cruel people; the world being critical of people who are sincerely religious; best of intentions often being misinterpreted; happiness not being a "*given*," and on and on and on. I sometimes think Brother John writes "out-of-body". Now, what do I mean by that? I think Brother John actually becomes the person. I mean everything! Brother John's characters have to come alive because he is the character. He is actually living it, not just passing through, not just experiencing it, but actually *living* it. He *is* the transvestite, the teenager in the pick-up truck, the old monk looking wisely back over his life, the newborn baby, the prostitute, the AIDS sufferer, the atheist, and all the other characters throughout this book. You can see them, hear them, feel them, touch them, smell them—even breathe with them. Just look at I REMEMBER ME; SUMMER: A SONNET; or AUTUMN: A SONNET. John's writing cannot be false. No one else would write what he does. No one else *could* write what he does. This alone makes his writing true. This does not have to be elaborated. It is understood that he is writing out of a higher knowledge, better said, a knowledge of higher things, a knowledge of God. However, many of the poems are of themselves not religious, but reflect John's sensitivity to nature and nature's beauty, as well as humanity and human beauty.

## POEMS OF WONDER AND PAIN

Brother John goes through phases, phases which are reflected in his poems. What do these phases mean? I'm not sure. I've seen the child, the teenager, the young man, the experienced monk. What is he now? What is he trying to be? Is he trying to prove something? What and to whom? Brother John realizes how much he has missed of life: the physical, even intimate part of life; the desire and sexuality of a mate; home; children; material things; all the things that a monk gives up. John's struggle is real. I have seen him suffer pain beyond any I have experienced, pain akin to the pain dramatized in BASKETBALL DIARIES, that horrible, horrible film about poet Jim Carroll's Catholic youth and lost innocence. John encouraged me to see this film because he thought it would help me understand him better. From what I've witnessed, John's pain is as great as Jim Carroll's, but John chooses to remain a faithful Catholic. I think John's pain is greater than that of anyone I've ever met. I have witnessed what happens when John works through the pain, whatever it is that causes him to suffer. I've also witnessed the joy, the abandonment to the present moment, the excitement. See his amazement over the beauties of life itself in THE FIREFLY SWIMS. Listen to John's wonder over a blade of grass in SOLEMN PROFESSION: A RETREAT, and you will hear the poetic voice of William Blake. John loves life and he loves loving. He lives to love other people although he will never admit it. His poems are the gift of himself to others. Read LOVE, DREW, and know how truly bonded this monk is with his little friend (born February 21, 1989). What is it that haunts me about the poem, COME TO ME, SWEET LYDIA? John is not always easy to know or to get along with. He can be difficult, even impossible. He can be arrogant, selfish, rude, even demanding at times. Maybe this is his way of masking deep hurts from the past. He is also kind, gentle, generous, compassionate and all the other things you would expect a monk to be, as you yourself would like to be. He's everything at once. John is John. I marvel at him. Does John's monastic life limit his poetic vision? Or, put differently, does John's writing limit his monastic life? I consider Brother John a religious writer because of who he is and what he is—a monk. Flannery O'Connor is a southern writer whom John greatly admires. She once said she dreaded a miracle cure of her lupus because she wanted to suffer for God. Brother John believes that as a Catholic we all should face the truth down to the worst of it. John is not afraid of facing the truth. He does not deny the struggle. He does not run from the pain. He's not afraid of the worst of it; he goes to the depth of the fear (or the worst of it) and beyond. He fears nothing. Yet, if I were to ask him, he would not see himself as fearless. He would say he was riddled with anxiety. Do we admire this self-scrutiny or does it scare us? It seems to me John's fearlessness comes from his being religious. I cannot discuss this because it is beyond me. Being "religious" is something intensely personal. Brother John does not go around shouting he is a Christian. You either are or you are not. You know! God knows!

## LINES OF DEPTH AND PROFOUND INTIMACY

Brother John's poetry seems very deep. I have read it over and over and many times have read it aloud, as all great poets suggest we do. So much of it seems to have been written in anger instead of love and then love instead of anger. What a complex person and writer is John! His writings are argumentative, confrontational, strident and provocative. Yes, John also has a great sense of humor. Surprised? I was! His humor ranges from satire to brief witticisms, half-*koans* and nonsense verse, even cynical parodies on religious life, such as LIFE WITH THE CRAZIES. Most of Brother John's poems are not funny poems; they are deep and serious and probably reflect a sadder side of life. A funny one is TOO MUCH COMPLEXITY KILLED THE CAT. How can you not laugh just reading the title; however, the author tells me this is actually a poem about suicide. FALSE HOPE is one of my favorite poems, a very tender and romantic poem. I see this as a woman's poem. A monk wrote this? I find a poem such as THE TRIAL OF EMMETT CLEMENT CLERIC CLOWN, too long and tedious. This could have been written as a short story, not a poem. Nonetheless, it is the way the author wrote it and wanted it to be presented—a long poem in rhyming couplets. Actually, John wrote it as a one-act play. When John speaks of his friends, I feel his intensity as he does so. His friends are such a part of him. I hear it in his voice and see it in his eyes when he speaks of them. He has introduced me to the most important relationships of his life. A number of John's poems express his capacity for warm, even intimate friendships, with women, men and children. Many who realize how rewarding a friendship with a monk can be hold a special place in their hearts for him. John's friends love him deeply, of this there is no doubt. A number of Brother John's poems express the profound intimacy he has experienced in his friendships with other men, some younger than he. Due to his many years in the seminary and the many years in the monastery, Brother John has developed an understanding of and sensitivity to persons with homosexual orientation. Brother John Albert's poems reflect the actual yearning on his part to be compassionate toward others and to live vicariously through them. Therefore, we can read his poems on many levels of meaning.

## UNSETTLING WORDS AND IMAGES

Other poems seem to express the author's dissatisfaction with himself, even an envy or jealousy toward those he regards as attractive and seemingly so much alive in their situations. John tends to glamorize what his friends see as ordinary. I feel this says more about who John actually is than anything else in my Introduction. My least favorite poem is COME HOME WITH ME. It leaves me feeling unsettled, my mind filled with images I don't understand. I just suffer through this one. The characters just keep going and going as if there's no end in sight. Does the poem ever resolve itself? To me, it does not. Maybe this is a "guy's" poem. The author seems to be in touch with many elements that society would consider decadent, even perverse. Here Brother John is not unlike other writers, poets and rock stars such as Bob Dylan and Jim Morrison. The influence of Dylan's TARANTULA and other stream of consciousness compositions is evident in SAINT JOHN'S STEEPLE and ONLY LONELY *"GOOD NIGHT,"* ONE MORE TIME SAY I, as well as the more explicit poem such as "AIN'T THIS BOB DYLAN'S BLUES AGAIN?" John's poems do not frighten me; however, I do think some of them are very deep, dark and maybe even destructive. He has been told this by others. I'm not sure if John seems to end some of his poems on a negative note. I just don't see a happy ending. Nonetheless, Brother John states: *"As a man, as a Christian, as a Roman Catholic, and as a Cistercian Monk, I believe the final note is positive while each poem is a self-contained entity where the characters are seemingly destructive and conquered by the forces of darkness. In the end Christ's love and light overcome everything else. This is the whole meaning of my life and the purpose of my writing: to make this truth of our redemption, despite ourselves, better known."* Working closely with John's art as I do, I read this sentiment in so many of his poems. It really comes through! Is there a sense of mystery in John's writings?  To me, all of John's poems start in Mystery, remain in Mystery, and end in Mystery.  But, of course, we are talking about something higher, more profound, and of greater depth.  We are talking about Mystery as human life in relation to divine life:  the reality of death; the reality behind ordinary appearances;  and the ultimate meaning of life as we know it.  Despite my negative judgment against some of his poems, I feel all of Brother John's poems are beautiful, even the ugly ones.

## PORTRAITS IN RHYME

How would I summarize Brother John?  This can be done in four words; he always wants more.  He wants more life, more knowledge, more experience as a man, more holiness as a monk—just more, more, more of everything!  I finally know what a "touchstone" is; Brother John is mine.  I love who I am and what I am when I am with him.  You would feel the same about yourself.  Brother John just has that special and unique gift.  It is an honor and a joy that Brother John Albert, OCSO, asked me to write this Introduction.  It speaks highly of our friendship that he wanted me to write it and felt I knew him well enough that I could write it.  I would like to repeat something I said in my Introduction to EARLY ESSAYS:  *"As a non-Catholic, working with Brother John certainly has been an exciting learning experience for me.  He has introduced me to the Psalms, Vespers, Compline and Holy Thursday.  By way of his friendship and his love for God, I am seeing a beauty that I did not know existed and experiencing an inner peace for which I was totally unprepared.  Thank you, John."*  I know the monk.  I know his writings.  Introducing Brother John to you has been a labor of love.  He is quite an extraordinary man.  When you have read this book, you will know something of the man, the monk and the writer.  Isn't he remarkable?  Brother John Albert, OCSO, himself, is the "portrait" in every rhyme.

Sue Loman, President
The Honey Creek Poets Society
159 Rue Fontaine
Lithonia, Georgia 30038

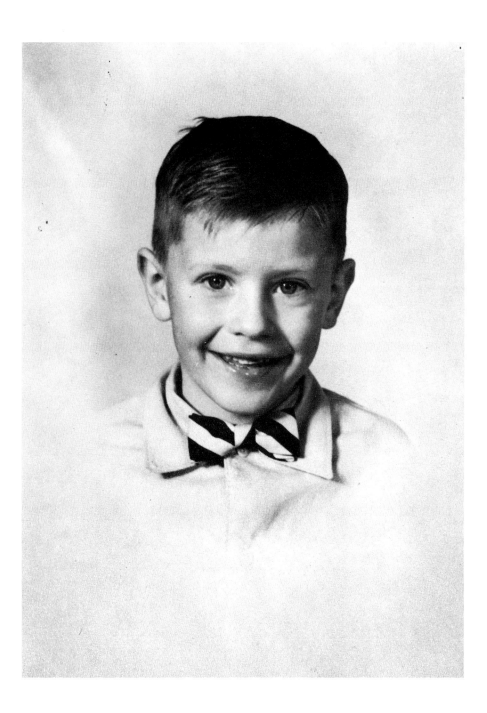

*"I have now tried to arrange the poems, as far as possible, in chronological order, the order in which they were written. . .I have tried to establish a chronological order, because many of the poems are so personal that, in their fragmentary fashion, they make up a biography of an emotional and inner life."*

D. H Lawrence
THE COLLECTED POEMS
12 May 1928

# PORTRAITS IN RHYME

# ORIENTATIONS: BY WAY OF A PREFACE

## I.

### 1.

Subterranean vibrations from the Masters of Japan
Telegrams from the unconscious
Penguin Mary writes her book of goose-step exercises
in the dark
escapes into the *Sesshu*
landscape
Shoot your mitres through with gold
See the tapestry from the other side
Undo the stitches of your *rakusu*
see the Easter egg in the Philosophers' tree
leave your glove up at German Ridge
Yours in the *Zen* Papacy
hard on the *frescoes*
another crown in my star
mitigated mystics hesychasts
Pulaski Skyway aperture cardiognasts

### 2.

Sing the "Schooner Juice Blues"
Keep a flea in a stick-match box
Realize your "Guardian Angel" wears earth shoes
Wear a hat like a tribute to the "beards in Brooklyn,"
Hassidim
Tame the lion with strokes
Take him

### 3.

Red Barrel Inn
life by default
Barbary coast where Twiggy once kissed cousins
*"Sub specie Infirmitatis"*
Saint Annie's Home and Grandma Mary
dear dead boy Tommy Putnam
Julian the Seminarian
Shannon's "Roaring 20's"

The Cottage Inn
Holyoke-East Washington Street A-go-go dancers
sway to "Get Back"
drinks come in half prices
make contact

4.

The Cafe Metropole and Greenwich Village the Albertine guru
nurse
Ravi Shankar's sitar gourd
the EPSILONS, THE PSY-KICKS; ONE COMPLEX REALITY
Mr. Gibson in a coat
of mahogany brown
with a country gentleman
companion with gold
buttons
Mr. Gretch Bass (voiced)
in curly blond
and music above
the glass-domes
dormitory
at night time
stars over
Tell city in the
southeast sky
and Jasper sparkling
in the north.

5.

dark and shining clarity
obscured by the light
quiescence
anxieties dream muses sigh
12 stringed tethered birds
a breeze in the tempest of the intelligence through the
tears over the years unmistakably Dylan
a touch of ermine
a touch of ebony
the stage of the electric Rimbaud
alchemy of X and Person
and Spirit

4

6.

tile dust and water patterns
similar piano *arpeggios*
parameters of an earlier existence
a delusion inside myself died because of your truth
the geologist and the astronaut
"Thin is in at the beach this year!"
*saguaro* cactus-*manzanitas*
bald-headed monk sees his reflection in the glass
window stars and constellations
sways to the music of another man's realities

7.

good bread is the key to a good sandwich
"Buy MONASTERY BREAD"
work was a ghost town today
can a porpoise chase a man-of-war?
every virus in our throats
the vagarious God
certainty is truth

8.

planets move like planes through the night
along long strands of angel's hair
flames set fire to my room
with bright lights and vibrations
I am awakened
configurations and lantern frames of memory
life's force and moon rises
constellation of feelings
conflagrations in the night like sunrises hiding
in the roots of moonlight
silence drapes like your great opera cape
of midnight velvet rimmed in white fur

9.

ah, the white satin lining of your sensitivities
ah, the double image of myself in the east window
glass as the moon is lifted from the
vest pocket of the night, grandfather's gold
pocket watch on a chain of stars and Venus bob
lights across the ridge of my memories

cars your jeweled bracelet sways
to the water-silk night of your black tendencies
Apotheosis Mind Guards Against The White Knight
Saint John's Steeple and Outtakes on Life
gold montage of your eyes and ermine

10.
could it be your tears are mine
from distance?

# II.

1.
A cycle of high school and college love songs:
electric guitars and clarinets, the squares,
the bohemes, the beats, the folks, the rocks,
the hype, the yippies, the freaks.  Ransacked,
wretched shack hospice, Niagara's kitchen.
Vietnam and Civil Disobedience.  President Johnson
at Monument Circle.  Sadness at the passing of time,
yet hoping in Thoreau's new Dawn.

2.
HIGHWAY 61, Dylan's sociological masterpiece, a
map of modern despair.  Americana c. 1965-1974.
Blood will flow over your women and children,
Vatican Council II, turning thirteen, the sexual
revolution all at once.  Melancholy disenchantment,
seeing a priest-friend on the corner as the bus
pulled out.  Something stirring, you knew not what
it was in the wind that tousled your golden hair.
The way she lifted the sun-glasses to her forehead!
Lovely tears from lovely eyes, why did they give
her woe?  Recluse nun roamed about, deceiving, hating
to say no but doing so with ease.

3.
Dropping bread while serving the Archbishop.
Evocations and Parameters of an earlier Existence.
Chrism.  Charism.  Academic sinecure.  Posturing.
Substituting.  Promises and Power.  Power and Experience.

*Panache.* Panoply. Wearing my Grandfather's wedding collapsible
black silk top hat through the gothic corridors and to an encounter
weekend at Lincoln Trails Park: *"You are suffering from an excess of
celebration!"* Seminary essay on Friendship as "light switch." The
late-night walks back under the stars. Sun reflecting off the Breviary's
gold edges in the sunset.

4.

Encounter with other cultures: the ivory features of the Greeks
captured in alabaster statuettes, English prints like
Dickens's London given to a friend, left behind and scattered
to the wind, prints of Highlanders and tartans. Learning from the
*TAO* to "give up learning." *"Do you take pride in your
self-knowledge?"* Attempting to build tabernacles around
fading hierophanies. *Ming* Dynasties. *Migne* Patrologies.
*DENZINGER.* Mondrian dreams. Yoga postures seen through
a mirror. *Zen* structures seen from within the mirror outward.

5.

Mind full of *KOAN*: "CHEW!" Watching him stand upon his
father's grave in the land of the Shawnee, father to his
family, father to his spiritual sons and daughters. Brothers
in Christ's spirit. The tests of time and tears. LIFE
itself loomed above us, behind and ahead of us.

6.

Notes. Papers. Journals. Essays. Poems. Pre-studies,
*"Give them up because you already own them, possess them
for all Eternity!"* A *Zen* moment of grace: destroying the
paper personality to better myself. Tearing, tearing, shredding,
shredding, my versed past into something else. Seeing the torn
manuscripts soaking in the rain like Keats whose name
was writ on water. . .

7.

The little plum-cloaked monk in the medieval tapestry. Sea shells
from Florida. Pope Pius X Chapel at Holy Spirit Abbey. Sunsets
toward the Gulf of Mexico. This bruised reed, this wavering
flame reminiscent of ISAIAH and Jesus. Post-profession; Meinradian
liturgies. A fury of mist soothing the sleepy eyes. Color blindness.
Whispers and silence in the cloister garden. Fire and freezing.
Facing the inner violence. Sometimes screaming. A release of the

evil spirits. The rustling of the crippled. The canes of the
unseeing. The footprints vanishing from the clay tiles.

8.

Recollections of friends, alive and gone to another existence.
*Concerdi laetiti* 13th century music for the soul. She, little
as we were, wore a plaid cape. She was a pure as a child's
toe. *"Do you want some food?"* *"I don't need any,"* he said.
It perhaps was just a paper moon with a hot dog and Ne-Hi
journey after all. Rod Stewart's "Reason to Believe" along
Seneca Park. WE FIVE: *"You were on my mind."* Chris Montez:
"The more I see you. . ." His mother always told him: *"Beware
of Kings bringing gifts from the East."* At night we sat at
a swing in a park. Afterwards you came looking for me: *"I
knew you probably were lonely and wanted to talk."* Lights
around the Capitol and District Heights. Sensitivity: *"Nothin'
but a heartbreak every night."*

9.

The recognized elements of Trappist life: mechanical noise
and material ugliness. Watermelon seeds swimming in the
plastic tray pool. *Ficus nekabudu* and *oshi-beni* making this
a *Zendo*. Reading JOB and carrying the processional cross on
All Souls Day. Forest in a white cloud T-shirt. Evenings of
memories and images of friends. Little T distributing palms,
one year after my Profession, missed but in prayer. "*Domine,
omnia nosti. Tu scis quia amo te. Ego scio quia tu amas me.*"
Hoping to say "YES!" to the proddings of His will. By blessed
cauldron flames, heralding the starry night: *"Christ, Our
Risen Light!"*

10.

Incursions back into Babylon. Atlanta. Piedmont Park sunset
amidst the red traffic lights. Dialoguing with Heraklitos
at the Waffle House. BLONDE ON BLONDE all-night girls out
on the escapade in Hartsfield Airport. Computer voices and
electric guitar apostates at Little Five Points. Discovering
the Old New York Book Shop. Being adopted by PWA'S.

11.

To renounce being an *impresario* of religion. To fear failure
but to forgive the failing. Not to protect ourselves to the
detriment of God's work. To be wary of evidence of success;
proficiency, even adequacy, are illusive in the work of God.
Right and power are often perceived in reverse, most often
hidden. To unmask the master of evasion within. Oh, God:
*Non Nisi Te! Viva Gesu!*

13.

In praise of criticism. Use these poems to start a marshmallow
roast. Words crackle in the fire of happy associations.
Whatever it is within these covers which is invaluable, it
is you and me.

# III.

1.

To the contemplative in us all:
You must become steeped in the ways
of non-reading. Do not read this
book. Experience it
Nothing that appeals to the contemplative
is ever useful: that is the secret
of their sanity. Contemplation
is valued uselessness.
Emptiness is Fulness.
Fulness is Emptiness.

2.

Truth is One. All of us speak
to the One. The All and Everything
is here. It comes from beyond us
and from within us.

3.

Things change and things stay the
same. Love experienced is never
forgotten. Love experienced is never
remembered: it is always in the present.

4.

You fantasize yourself in cowl and austere
beauty when you are tired of your life or
feeling prayerful. Your mind is the matrix
of reality and delusion. Put flesh on it.
Cast it not in black and white. Live in
the paradox and the compromise. Grow into
your own.

5.

Grace is a sort of continual mist in
the hothouse of contemplation. The
school of contemplation is the combination
of the catastrophic and the calisthenic.
Only the apathetic drop out. The way out
is inward. The more you think about how little
you think of it, the more significant *it* becomes.

6.

You are the vortex through which you *experience*
all others. We are the vortex through which you
*experience* yourself. I *experience* all others
through you. You *experience* all others through me.
Your heart: restless, strong, always wanting
something better for us all.

7.

When you say you *would* not like yourself, that
means you *do* not like yourself. Shame is the name
you give to your own sense of inadequacy and
unworthiness. Do not continue to lacerate yourself.
Pain itself is not the means of self-appropriation.
Develop the capacity to contain your own anxiety.
Wherever you are, be happy doing what you do well.

8.

Illness is the gift of the strong to the weak.
Health is the gift of the group to the one. Lasting
health is the gift of God to none. Being a legend
at early death is better than a bad reality in later
life. What an option!

9.

Nobody owes a *thing* to anybody. Nobody
responds to need by neediness. The terms
of your acceptance are defined by what others
are allowed to do. Only the unpopular preoccupy
us. Know the price of popularity. Rejection is
the reward for being unpopular. Only those who
are truly free are unpopular. The choice is
made for you. Pride is the storehouse of all
things. Works of mercy are the last refuge of
those who need to be needed. The needy despise
the needed. Popular devotions are the last refuge
of those who have a need to please. The pure in
intention are pleased by God.

10.

There is no place for politics in the contemplative
life. Politics is the exercise of power within a
locked-up system. Contemplation transcends all
systems. Power is a drug. Contemplation is clean
living. Everyone is in disguise. It all comes
out in the verse.

# PART ONE:  PRE-MONASTIC POEMS

1965 - 1974

# LIKE A CLOWN

Here I am all alone
by the telephone
laying 'round
like a clown
feelin' blue

What to do?
Wait for a call from you

Here I am so forlorn
by the telephone
laying 'round
like a clown
feeling blue

Guess I'll call
someone new!


# UNIVERSITY SCENE:  A FRAGMENT

the University
the lakes
the dome
the grotto
the swans


# THE HUMAN VOID

Indian Pandit sitaring West
4 long-haired Englishmen turning East
Amplified folk-artist bucking society
Shakespearean Welsh-bard singing about love
White-robed Pontiff preaching about Peace
Black-robed nuns fingering their beads
Fathers trying to communicate with their sons.

## BERTHA HAGGARDY

Bertha Haggardy
lives in everybody
else's world.

She tells them
what to do.
She tells them
what to say.
She tells them
how to act.

Bertha, Bertha,
don't you know
that's wrong.
Bertha, Bertha,
don't you know
that's wrong.

Bertha Haggardy
lives in everybody
else's world.


## DREAMING THE DAY AWAY

As I looked in the distance I could see
A castle that was so pretty.
I wanted to make it my home for I stood but all alone.
But then I knew I could not stay.  I must return another day.
Dreaming the day away-ay-ay.  Dreaming the day away.

And as I looked in the sky above I saw a little white dove.
It stood for Peace and for Love.
But not today.  Not this way.
Dreaming the day away-ay-ay.  Dreaming. . .

And as I looked both East and West
I saw only War and Unrest.
And then I remembered that little castle
Far from this turmoil and battle.
Dreaming the day away-ay-ay. Dreaming. . .

Now I live in that little castle
Far from all turmoil and battle.
And through you say it isn't true
I can only invite you to
Dream the day away with me. Dreaming the day away.


## THE CALL

The start is now ten years away,
but I still hear it every day.
And though I try I can't deny,
That I know it's here to stay.

One time I was Kelly green,
O Come, to me it had bidden.
I even drove up on the curb,
In answer to the word.

I thought I had time to spare,
But really I was nowhere.
My heart was so strongly pierced,
And it was gray all around me.

And now the Future seems so long,
And oh I wish that I were wrong.
But though I try I can't deny,
That I know it's here to stay.

Please give me an answer.
Tell me that I'm wrong.

## SQUIRE TOM

Oh, young lad named Squire Tom,
you work for your Master all day long.
Do all that's asked of you,
Oh, Squire Tom.

The Morning's rays that start your day,
match your Master's heraldry.
Never be caught out of sight.
Oh, Squire Tom.

Clean and polish smooth breast-plate,
sharpen lance and sword and mace.
Comb and stroke soft helmet plume,
Oh, Squire Tom.

After working hard all day,
then it's time for you to play.
Someday a Master you will be,
Oh, Squire Tom.


## LIEUTENANT SAMUEL HARDING

Lieutenant Samuel Harding was such a gallant soldier.
Everyone said he was born to be a military man.
He was always brave and strong, tall and so handsome.
And the girls always raved about his curly yellow-brown hair.

And when the Civil War came he chose the side of the Gray.
He was given a position in the Virginia Calvary.
He wore a bright gray uniform trimmed in yellow and red.
He wore a dashing army cap smartly upon his head.

He fought for his own family.  He fought for his own land.
In every battle he was an inspiration for every other man.
He led his troops in campaigns, won victories wherever they went.
He was always the pride of his regiment.

18

And when the war was ended, no more shot and shell,
The Lieutenant returned home to marry a pretty Southern belle.
They started a life together, never a thought of parting.
And so happily ends my story of Lieutenant Samuel Harding.


# THE WOMAN CLOTHED WITH THE SUN

REVELATION 12

Once there appeared this great wonder,
a Woman clothed with the sun.
She stood with the moon under her heels,
wearing a twelve-starred crown.

And there appeared another wonder,
a Dragon great and red,
with seven heads and twelve large horns,
a crown upon each head.

The Dragon drew the other star,
he cast them to the earth.
He then stood before the Woman,
ready to give birth.

The Woman fled into the wilderness,
ere safe from harm.
She loved and fed and served her God,
the Child in her arms.

For thirty years the child grew,
He grew to be a man.
He then suffered and died;
to win our Redemption.

Rejoice and be glad all you people,
the Dragon is conquered.
Let us love and serve and adore,
Jesus Christ Our Lord.

## JOHN BARLEYCORN

He's always as popular as he can be.
Always is at a party.
There's no need to feel down
when you know that he's around.

Always time to draw a line.
Always feelin' good and fine.
Laughter, have a good time!
John Barleycorn comes to dine.
John Barleycorn,
You're so important!
John Barleycorn,
You're so important.


## SONG FOR HELEN BURNS

After reading Charlotte Bronté JANE EYRE

At Lowood it began.  Helen was her name.
She told me something new:

*"The love of God is true."*
At Lowood it began.  Helen was her name.

At Lowood it began.  Helen was her name.
She told me something new.
She told me something true:
*"Do not be afraid.*
*I am going to die.*
*I am going to God."*
At Lowood it began.  Helen was her name.

At Lowood it began.  Helen was her name.
She told me something new.
*"The love of God is true.*
*It's for everyone."*
At Lowood it began.  Helen was her name.

At Lowood it began.  Helen was her name.
Helen was her name.  Helen was her name.


## IF YOU EVER NEED ME

If you need me, I'll be right here.
If I can't love you, I'll just wipe your tears.

The meaning of Love is something to give,
To make Life much more pleasant to live,
To show that I'm here to fulfill your needs.
Oh, if only you could do this for me.

You're always so happy, so laughin' and gay.
I find it hard to find a pretty day.
You're always so joyful, cheerful and bright.
Couldn't you share some of your light?

Now I know it.  It's clear to see.
You couldn't possibly love a guy like me.
I know my purpose.  For me it's best—
To be right here when there's no one else.

If you need me, I'll be right here.
If I can't love you, I'll just wipe your tears.


## UNDER THE BUBBLE

You've got to stop your cryin'.
You've got to stop your sighin'.

Come on and wipe those tears.
You've got to kill those fears.

Wave good-bye to the blues.
You've got nothin' to lose.

I've got Charlie on a string.
I'm into a brand new thing.


## I DON'T WANT IT

I don't want it.  I don't need it.
You can keep it for another man.

I don't want to hear it—the same old song
Just because you've got the blues?

Walk on out.  Go on by.
Get yourself another guy.


## CLOWN

Clown, clown,
clothes of rags
'round, 'round
watch you dance

Clown, clown
make us smile
head on ground
feet up high

Clown, clown
paint on face
top-hat round
sad frown chase

## FIRE EXTINGUISHER BLUES/OR LINES FROM A REJECTED POEM

"I don't want no shiny shoes.
I don't want a new suit blue.
When I feel the way I do,
All I want is you."

"When I'm burning up inside
for you, you just throw water
on my feelings, toss sand in
my eyes, play refrigerator, dose
me out with your pouts and
persistent silence."

"I don't want no shiny shoes.
I don't want a new suit blue.
When I feel the way I do,
All I want is you."


## GRAVE OF THOMAS MERTON, GETHSEMANI ABBEY #1

A white flash through my mind at the clap of
thunder overhead. . .pounding eardrums and
then a sense of everlasting peacefulness. . .
nothing to be evaluated..death and life
were one.


## 125TH STREET RIDE

Do I want you to leave me
on a hot crowded street
in the blazing summer heat
of Harlem, New York City?

Driving in car at fast pace,
the sky's an ugly goo.
With my hand reach out to
touch the whole human race.

I sense loss.  I sense hate
in a city too big to live.
Is there anything I can give
or is it just too late?

I sense hunger.  I sense pain.
People crawling like ants,
living with garbage and rats.
But we're happy just the same!


## FROM THE BENCH

amber hour sunset
on your face in
waiting interstate
traffic
giddiness
screaming "bitch"
to release
the tension
blood scattered
all over the walls
of consciousness
a little won K
how fond we were
in the snowfall
of our parting

## BROTHERS' PARADISE

Standing at the edge of a drop-off. . .a "wiping away"
of ordinary awareness. . .all reality as one. . .the
grayness and dampness of the Wednesday afternoon in
October, at 5:00 P.M. For an instant all made sense.

## CONLEY HALL

At night, in the darkness, I split in two, from head
to foot, and each side touched the opposite walls of
my room. I knew that I was gone, nothing else existed
of me. And then there was God. He too started
splitting in half and I was overcome by a tremendous
feeling of emptiness and terror. I got up from my
bed at great effort and went to the room of a friend
who was fortunately still awake.

## AT THE READING OF *EZEKIEL*

A feeling of tremendous hilarity. . .I wanted to
scream out the laughter but held back. Sanity and
insanity were not distinct.

## CHRIST THE KING CHURCH

I stood up to go to Communion. . .it seemed I was
walking on air. . .a sensation of being elevated far
above the heads of the other people. . .everything
meshed into One. . .kneeling back at my pew the tears
came. . .pain and joy were the same.

# SOMEWHERE BETWEEN *SATORI* AND TODAY:
# A *ZEN* GARDEN

Foolish me
to think
smooth sand and rough rock
misplaced, when within wooden box are found.

Foolish me
to think
furrows flow and
circles swirl
disjointly, when within wooden box go 'round.

Foolish me
to think
body, soul and
human heart
displaced, when near wooden box are found.

Wise me
to know
sand-rock, furrow
and soul
unite, when within and near wooden box are found.

    Nature, Her own Harmony.
    She seeks and herein She abounds.

## AUTUMN: A SONNET

Speak to me of what you do,
and  how you fill your days.
To spin do your fingers raise,
to gather yarn-yellow?
Then say to me of lonesome nights
how cold closes 'round.
Do you wear embroidered gown,
and sit by firelight?
Then state aloud your heart-felt wish,
the wish (I beg) to be with me?
Aft' all is wished come true to be,
then press your gentle kiss!
    Fear nothing, nothing my Dear,
    Fear nothing, find you your true love here.


## WINTER:  A SONNET

In the coming of the night when the wind blows cold,
think then on me as a friend of old.
As the moon rises high and the trees do sway,
remember how once I came to stay.
In the deep of the night when the stars do shine,
recall lovers' toast with goblets of wine.
As the fire burns bright and the shadows do loom,
remember how once I sang Love's tune.
In the coming of the morn when the darkness fades,
think then on me as I took my leave.
As the sun rises high and the birds do sing,
remember my promise to return again.
    In the coming of the night when the wind blows cold,
    Think then on me as a friend of old.

## SPRING: A SONNET

A metaphysic make you not,
of each experience true.
Beyond your mind you have a heart,
an intuition too.
More than to reason away,
the events of each hour.
Life is a joy from day to day,
each moment for your pleasure.
So stop your cares and stop your woes,
take time to breathe Spring air.
And let brook-water cool your toes,
ev'ning breeze tousle your hair.
   Life is a joy from day to day,
   Each moment for your pleasure.


## SUMMER: A SONNET

Forget me not, my Lady Dear,
When this Summer's gone.
When strains of song you no longer hear,
And leaves touch the ground.
Forget me not, my Lady Fair,
When to monk's life I go.
When God's praise choirs do declare,
And trees embrace the snow.
Forget me not, My Lady Love,
When this good life I leave.
When chimes the church-bell from above,
And blossoms mark my grave.
   Forget me not, My Lady Dear,
   When one day I am gone.

# FORGET ME NOT, MY LADY

Forget me not my lady
love, when Autumn leaves
touch the ground.

When . . .

Remember me my lady,
when from this life I'm gone.
When church bells ring from above,
and snow covers my tomb.


# IF MINE WERE BUT TO GIVE

Stringed instruments from Persia,
incense from Bengal.
Chinese silks for your pleasure,
and perfumes from Nepal.

Precious stained glass from Roma,
smooth wines from Paree.
Moroccan rubies for your own,
and rare books from Madrid.

Silver goblets from Mexico,
bracelets from Peru.
Canadian furs for your robes,
and California gold doubloons.

These and more I wish you, Love,
if mine were but to give.
Your beauty surpasses all above,
all that I could ever give!

## SATURDAY

Morning Song.
Sky barely cracking open to let slender ray of light in
to brighten rainy day.
Not snow, not sleet this Christmas time,
Yet Winter is truly here.
The Holiday festive-heart you must have
to spread good holiday cheer.

## FRIENDSHIPS

Friendships are born and
don't be surprised, so die
and so what!

Keep me from more webs
of illusion
of selfishness
of insane desire
and false hope.

Let people go on with their involvements
I am so tired
and choose to lie down
all activity
and all effort
and all others
I'm tired of the world's *débris*.

# DEATH

Death does not seem such a bad thing
if it will liberate me
from this dreadful condition
of the continual killing of myself.

A pathological psychic suicide
does not seem so strange
when a person is dead already
and there is nothing left but the decayed matter.

# TIME

Staggering, isn't it!
Time
Sometimes it does not last long enough,
Other times, it does not seen to end
Oh, the fleeting pleasure and the lingering emptiness!

Amazing, isn't it!
Time
Sometimes, more often, it seems against us
Oh, the inevitable, inescapable confinement of Time!

And, Space
Interesting, isn't it!
Space
Can be transcended by mind
Yet conditions remain and still prevail
Oh, the inexplicable illusion of being free from Fate!

# A SOLDIER'S REMINDER HOME:  TELEGRAM HOPE

Time was
when you and I
were together, gladly
and joy filled our hearts as merry-song filled the air.

Time is
now you and I
are parted, sadly
and sorrow fills our hearts and merry-song no longer heard.

Time will be
when you and I
will be united, madly
and joy will fill our hearts as merry-song fills
the air (once again).

    Crazy wars no longer will be declared.  And, my love,
    children from our insanity will be spared.


# OF EARLY YEARS

Oh, the violence in some men's hearts!
And this inane (insane) war in Vietnam
Continues on
Incessantly.

Oh, Youthful Idealism, Peace!
Of early years
Given way now
To complacency and deeper enslavement
To selfish pursuits.

Now no longer on peer group praise
But on my own convictions I must stand.
And are they much anymore?

# SATURDAY WALK FOR CONSCIENCE

Songs
People
Peace in the hearts of some.

It's not easy!
And some people have come
the hard way—through the
Desert.
And the crossing hasn't ended yet.

Monk, priest, minister, men, women
Students, the old, the
young on Coronation Day.


# MY LIFE IS A PENDULUM

My life is a pendulum
a chain-swing from joy to dread.
Feelings of change come
with the thoughts of my life led.
I love God but am from Him far.  I am what I do and
From my ways I cannot part.
But my life is always good:  in intentions.


# FIND NOT FAULT

Find no fault in human deeds.
What more can one man do to fill another man's needs?
For love, friendship and understanding too.
This man sets out his best to do!

And if you find me not strong,
And caught within my own self-wrongs,
Please take time to remember that I'm a man,
And doing the best I can.

And rest assured that in my eye,
The same measure to you applies.
Why sorrow when what is good is done,
By you and me and honest men!


## AND THEN YOU ARE GONE

the hansom cab lamps
disappear through the
dark night pines
and then you are gone


## BASILICA CHURCH: ABBEY OF GETHSEMANI, KENTUCKY

In this church I am able to experience peace, a real exposure to God. The fear
of facing myself seems not so forceful here and for a minute the Truth is
breaking through. Of all the things in the world to be, I want to be a monk.
Merton has taught me that I am to live out my vocation according to my unique
calling, the unique calling of personal response demanded from each man.
Today thoughts of friend Dan Wessler, such a man of peace whom I am so
fortunate to know. A tour with Father Davis and a chat with Brother Cassian.


## IN THE ROOM OF A FRIEND

Spent the night here in the room of a friend who is away. It is good to get out
of my own familiar setting, even if only for a little while. I have come here to
confront myself in a way that I would not while in my own room. First real *Zen*
sitting in quite some time. Difficult to center but deep concentration once begun.
Generally, thoughts of friendships, images and faces passing. Sense of peace,
real love for others. Realization that I must sustain relationships. The wish to
be a monk comes through, a look into the depths of my being. Eventual
breaking into prayer the deeper I got, lost sight of self and counting as dialogue
with Jesus began, sense of expanding, large head and nose on top of a small
distant body.

## ST. MEINRAD WALK: 4:00 A.M.

The stars were bright last night as I walked around the buildings. What a strange sight to see my light the only one on and such a strange sound—my footsteps upon the ground. There was real peace in the night and my mind was swept clear by the wind.

\*

Walking under the stars bright
late last night,
there was nothing left
but you.

Full of sorrow and pain and
my self-shame,
there was nothing left
but you.

And where was I to turn for joy
if not to you?
And there was nothing left
but you!

All lights out
late last night,
there was nothing left
but YOU.


## ST. LEO ABBEY: ST. LEO, FLORIDA

The caterpillar claws
of the orange groves
at sunset cast me into the silence
struck speechless by the beauty

## PIECES OF NATURE

woodpeck tadpole peacock fan

## LAST NIGHT

the lovely stars watched
last night
as I shone brightly

## EASTER VIGIL: HOLY SPIRIT ABBEY, CONYERS, GEORGIA

Late sleepy April hour
far-come pilgrim found
by blazing festive fire
close together bound
above whose heads there 'rose
lone flame of paschal light
from men in whitened robes
a cry broke the night:
*"Light of Christ!"*

One early April morn
close-bound Christians found
at break of Easter dawn
making their glorious sound:
*"Jesus Christ lives on."*

# COME TO ME, SWEET LYDIA

Come to me, Sweet Lydia,
while moonbeams light the path
and each the next star shines prettier
together we'll be at least

Come silent then through the night
while the breeze blows so warm
slowly like the clouds that glide
to tease me with your charm

# THE TRIAL OF EMMETT CLEMENT CLERIC CLOWN: A ONE-ACT PLAY IN VERSE

*"Truly, truly, I say to you, unless a grain of wheat falls into the earth and dies, it remains alone; but if it dies it bears much fruit."* JOHN 12:24

\*

Each Christian has as his task the living-out of this Gospel parable and parabolic it indeed is. When a man attempts to actualize his own spiritual death in Jesus he soon realizes that he is doing nothing more than preserving his 'old self'. Christian death is not under his control. It will come from without. It will bring with it sorrow and anger, resignation and, ultimately, true peace. You, reader, are about to hear the voices of yet another man's confrontation with this Gospel parable. Perhaps you will find in these words hints of others, perhaps whispers of your own confrontation with this same Gospel parable. If these voices should lead you closer to ultimate peace, I am happy with you.

\*

*Dramatis Personae:*

Popo Bozo, Archbuffoon:   Grand Inquisitor, Mouth-piece for ecclesiastical residue left over from the years before individuation.

Histis Mistis, *Advocatus Diaboli:*  For the prosecution, the ever-present whisper of doubt, confusion and self-contempt.

Digmor Klossli, Clinician:   For the detection, the high-pitched tones of a hypercritical questioning.

*Karuna,* Defensor Clementi:  For the detection, the soft speech of inner peace and growing self-acceptance.

Emmett Clement, Cleric Clown:  The one tried, subject of the perennial quest and object of the accusations.

\*

Popo Bozo: in god's name we pray be we guided through this day
god's task we take to hand defend it in the land
one way there is we know and so we're here to show
god's way will never go protect the *status quo*
commence then the hearing

Histis Mistis: your foolishness before your gracious face a most
serious case I place that of Emmett Clement Cleric Clown
now a man of some renown charged with willful motive to
monkish life devote him now to witness official clinician
to share with us his intuition and sound conclusions too

Digmor Klossli:
Emmett Clement Cleric Clown you paint your face
to hide a frown father fearer phantasy freak sex-repressed
hostility streak constrained restrained compulsive kid
neuro-neurotic-psychotic schiz normally abnormal but
more do i see there is still something up your sleeve and
this i cannot perceive

Histis Mistis:
Emmett Clement Cleric Clown more of your strangeness
i have found bedspread vestment black-jap stole navel gazer
what a show Emmett Clement yes we see the mask you wear is
up *zen* sleeve incensed tea set black-*zafu* seat Jesus hater
what a feat foolishness my case i rest

Popo Bozo: most shocking it is true let us seek another clue
speak then the defense

*Karuna*: remember of old the apostle said
a special gift upon each head
is given for the common good
in loving service to the Lord
and so with Emmett Clement

Popo Bozo: more confusing it is getting
perhaps there's someone we're neglecting
speak then Emmett Clement Cleric Clown.

Emmett Clement:  *dogen* not am i nor francis of assisi
yet i am what you do not see the i am you
think i should be i am none but the i am
i am i am me.

Histis Mistis:  Emmett Clement would you please
stop remarks so silly as these

Popo Bozo:  hold quick your tongue histis mistis
your turn in time on this i insist
continue then Emmett Clement
but on the puzzles please relent

Emmett Clement:  sitting on the floor
waiting for something to happen
little did i realize that *satori* had come
i went to play the guitar
and it was already playing of itself

Popo Bozo:  *defensor Clementi karuna* come
speak to us of what he's done
these puzzles are unending

*Karuna*:  o foolishness how much i dread
to speak out loud of what i've heard
for righteous sake i pray
let this man have his say

Popo Bozo:  speak then Clement Clown
what you say be written down
with each word your cause you plead

Emmett Clement:  the day was darker than my darkest night
the sun was blood red a bleeding hole low
in the vapored side of the leaded sky
coal trees cracked through torn nerves
in skin mists the steam rose the heat increased
no man dared stir creatures took flight
all gripped by the fingers of a terrible fright
tensed their stance in the wake of immanent doom
not a word was heard neither a sign
it was the stillness of a man about to die

and then from somewhere in the far-off bounds
hardly heard but a ghastly sound whick whack whooh
god must it be the lash of a whip held by
a man strangely hid
yet each man knew in his trembling heart
that never such tremors did a whip impart
whick whack whooh whick whack whooh
the last blood ray dripped from the swollen sky
as the stinking steam continued to rise
and the stifling heat grabbed the breath
from gasping throats whick whack whooh
god how could it be a reaper's blade about to slash whick
with all men hid whack
and day time past whooh
then through thick vapors they caught the sight
on nature's edge against the sky a blackened form
with pleated robe and hooded head
in upraised arms a thrashing blade
whick whack whooh whick whack whooh
the time to cry had long passed by
no movement could be made as the cold sweat cruel surgeon's
knife slit their faces
Whick Whack Whooh Whick Whack Whooh
before their eyes doom figure's blade Whick
took Whack its vengeful Whooh toll
to his feet fell weeds and wheat
and all else that stood WHICK WHACK WHOOH
but then they wrenched by horror struck WHICK WHACK WHOOH
in utter disbelief WHICK at the sight of WHACK
well-hid man WHOOH lying hacked at his feet
the blood-bath unending went Whick Whack Whooh

until all lay dead whick whack whooh
i the only to escape whick whack
god's hand upon my head whooh

Popo Bozo:  more perplexing than anything I have ever heard
come to me your woeful words Clement
much spirit there is in the wheels you are turning
but for clarification i am yearning
let us from others hear

41

Histis Mistis:  foolishness this man is guilty of consorting
with the mad man run to the east holy church's
sacral authority and her high holy feasts
are secretly here rejected disguised as weeds and wheat
and such a sorry fate for church's holy saints
how can he carry the name Christian?

Digmor Klossli:  archbuffoon and all good men look beyond
what you see before you multi-*magno* maladjustment find
plasto-phallic pathologic *fugue* elasto-castric anxieties hide
behind transference devised blade that sliced
manly weeds and womanly wheat fallen to psycho-sexual oedipal feet

*Karuna*:  this 'night' should surely see something born in each
of us hearing all that is good crying out to be recognized
there are some things man can do and others he must let be
remember scripture's saying and leave this man to his way
with his winnowing fan in hand he will search through the land
with chaff he will feed his fire the wheat he will pile higher
upon his threshing floor

Popo Bozo:
o noble spokesman while you spoke i was being most distracted
by a curious sound from near 'round the sound of someone lashing
be so good put me at ease cast a gaze outside would you please

Histis Mistis:
o archbuffoon it cannot be what my lips say that my eyes see
while Clement spoke i thought it a joke just a scripture story
my god what is that looms but blackened figure of doom
the heretic Emmett told god's truth but why so ghastly a proof

Digmor Klossli:
o foolishness you must not look upon the pleated robe and
head with hood while Clement spoke i thought it a ploy
to me deceive and reality distort whick whack whooh whick whack
whooh what you heard was not a lash WHICK WHACK WHOOH WHICK
WHACK WHOOH this confused Clown told no lies but why
did he not WHICK WHACK warn us WHOOH

The last words spoken on trial day came from the compassionate
*Karuna*. They were words of encouragement to strengthen his beloved
Emmett Clement the Cleric Clown at the final moment:

EMMETT CLEMENT CLERIC CLOWN
YOU HAVE FACED THE DAILY PAINS AND THE LIFE-LONG TRIAL
YOU HAVE NOT ASKED FOR THESE HUMILIATIONS
THEY ARE GIFTS
FEAR NOT DEATH IT WILL BRING WITH IT THE
POSSIBILITY OF LIFE
IT IS THE GREATEST GIFT
AND FROM WHERE AND WHOM COULD SUCH DISASTROUS GIFTS
COME BUT GOD
DIE AND PUT ON YOUR MONK'S ROBE

## ANOTHER CROWN

a cloud of stars
another crown in my star


## AN EPISODE IN THEOLOGY CHAPEL

A sunflower, opening whirling, spinning, bringing me to its center. . .I could hardly stand to receive the Eucharist. . .Turning to receive. . .Coming back I looked into the eyes of a friend and at once everything made sense. . . a terrific feeling of ease. . .my worries disappeared and I could hardly restrain myself for my joy.


## TURTLE TEARS

Today the turtle
laid four eggs
and shed many more tears


## SAN FERNANDO VALLEY, CALIFORNIA #1

*saguaro* trees
*yucca*
desert
spring
crescent moon

# THE OLD MAN AND THE LAMP

At twilight time one warm eve, the old man came to sight
on nearby hill clearly seen, he stood with lantern light
far he held above his head the Lamp of *Dharma* Truth
a beacon bright for my path a light of constant proof

I watched with awe as he swayed, the beam he turned to me
a light to see on my way, a guide to endless peace
slowly then he moved his hands and held the lantern lower
the movement caused me to stand, to catch the fading glow

To tease it seemed with his sleeve he hid the beacon beam
from the hill he took his leave and then no more was seen
searched for him in great dismay yet nothing more I saw
than hilltop trees, swayed by the breeze and setting evening star.


# IMAGES OF SAINT MEINRAD

I used to walk on rainy days,
along paths of wet pine needles.
And catch a glimpse along the way,
of distant Abbey steeples.

Near a bridge there was a shrine,
of carpenter and son.
And there for hours I would hide,
and play for them my tunes.

I used to walk on misty nights,
close by the church clock tower.
And listen closely for the chimes,
that marked the midnight hour.

Some days I'd go to chapel shrine,
to chase November gloom.
Or take along a friend and wine,
to watch May flowers bloom.

Near the church there was a garden,
with fountains and rock ledges.
And there I sat lost in thought,
hidden by the hedges.

Some nights I'd pace the cloister court,
when all had gone to bed.
And whisper a question to my Lord,
about what lay ahead.


## THE LITURGY OF THE HOURS ACCORDING TO *ZEN*

Each day I go walking South
morning sunglow falls about
quickly goes my sleepy yawn
as Northern bird sings his song

Each night I sit facing West
as evening star takes her rest
lonesome sorrow passes by
as Eastern moon greets the sky


## *UNSUI* (Cloud and Water)

I along
go *angya*
march
on mushy
mud road
flippity
flip flop
flip-flops
for
my shoes
floppity flip
sopping
water

through
my
toes

rickety
wicker-ware
*ajirogasa* bonnet
bobbing on
my head
*kesa bunko*
box
bouncing
on my back

wind
whipped
ripped
*rakusu*
wrapped
'round
my
neck
flat sticky
palms
pattered
by
drip-drop
dripping
drop by
drop drop
rain

humming
high-pitched
hymn
in harmony
with
tinging
tight
electric
lines
taunting

my ringing
wringing
wet
ears

I along
go
mushy
mud road
chewing
chop by
chop chop
chippitty
chop
mindful
*koan*
question

big
rising
moonbeam smile
shining
through
my
boy-full
joyful
tears


## "COME TO THE COAST"

*"Come to the coast,"* coaxed the host.
*"Come to the land of enchantment."*

When the day grew short I rose to the thought
and took a ride beyond.

The land lay bare before the car
and I steered it to the edge of visibility.

## MY *KOAN* IS JESUS

My *koan* is Jesus
I chew it all day long


## SAN FERNANDO VALLEY, CALIFORNIA #2

Joshua trees silhouetted by the
setting sun


## LOS ANGELES INTERNATIONAL AIRPORT

I was searched at the gate
the gateless, electric gate


## ONBOARD 727 FOR SAN FRANCISCO

a time of uncertainty
the Midnight Flyer left at the wrong time
at 11:35 we were let on


## SAN FRANCISCO

Different people doing the same things

## SAY NO MORE TO ME

Say no more to me
of the times past spent
in quiet times of sleepy nights
and early morning suns

Say no more to me
of days gone by
when hill-top trees and
evening breeze brought us
such delight

Tell me now of our hurt
which seems to mar the past
and causes us to question love
and wonder: *"Will it last?"*


## AT NIGHT IT CHOKES ME

At night it chokes me
the throat lump of
swollen heart
that brings the
steady pain

Take the bittersweet
portion of life
that comes upon you
unexpectedly

Swallow it quickly
down
lest it choke you
with its poison.

## SANDIA CREST

O *Sandia*, how long must you tease us?
You lure us to your heights
and cast us to your depths.

You hold captive our eyes
raised high from afar,
and take to death young boy
who dared to play too near.

In you, *Sandia*, find we both
breathless life and breathless death.


## TOO MUCH COMPLEXITY KILLED THE CAT

*"Let Hercules himself do what he may, the cat will mew,
and dog will have his day."* HAMLET V:ii

\*

Too much complexity killed the cat.
Felix squirmed his way to death
(because) he got caught in the main thoroughfare
between self and not-self.
He died in the middle of the crossroad
between total despair and care for others.

The complexity killed him
right in the middle of the second act of the play,
the "PLAY OF DAYS" he called his life,
although it was never lived out,
his life that is.

The complexity killed him:
he could not make up his mind
to do what was good for him or to do what
was good for others.

51

They were not the same, you see,
at least not for him:
the complexity killed him,
the solution found him before
he found the solution.

They buried him:
on one side—the mouse of merriment gone wrong,
on the other—the dog of drudgery, worn out.

And on his stone they wrote:

"Complexity killed the Cat;
Curiosity carved the stone."


## SANTA FE, NEW MEXICO

Hold fast the words
molded in moments of hate
and without regret
you will greet the dawn.


## A TIME TO DEEPEN

A time to deepen rather than broaden


## WHATEVER I WANT TO DO

Whatever I want to do
I can do wherever I am

## AT THE HOME OF MY RELATIVES: GREENWOOD, INDIANA

Seems if I don't start living monastic life soon I never will. There is much of the "dust-wiping" tendency of *Shen-hsui* in my notion of monastic life: removing myself from people and things in an attempt to get back to the clarity, to the original beauty, the pristine purity of my being. So much self-analysis, self-scrutiny, is no longer productive. It is time to be, not to think about being what I want to be. My understanding of *Zen* has been that of the predecessors of *Hui-neng*, the "dust-wiping" *Ch'an*. Seeing now that *Sunyata* is the absence, not of certain conditions, but rather no clinging to any condition, principle, notion or idea. It is not even trying to cling to nothing. It is the statement that all is what it is, nothing more, nothing less.

## ON THE GREYHOUND BUS: NEAR SHAWNEETOWN, ILLINOIS

Nothing is to be attained.

## I WANT TO BE A MAN OF CHRISTIAN LOVE

I want to be a man of Christian love, living a
life of poverty and simplicity. I want to be a monk.

## AND SO I SIT QUIETLY IN ST. MARY'S CHURCH

And so it has come to pass: my friend is a priest. Twenty-six years of living, twenty years of formal education, loving and preparing, he is what he has wanted to be. It has been my great joy to be with this man through the time our friendship, during these last days of preparation and finally during the happy days of celebration.

And so I sit quietly in St. Mary's Church, Shawneetown, with *rakusu* on and with journal and pen in hand. I had to come back to this beautiful church one more time before leaving. Today it is empty and dark, in extreme contrast to the great gathering of last week. And it is good that things settle down a little bit for all of us. My friend still has the move to make, to transfer all his belongings and treasures to the Cathedral in Belleville. In my heart I rejoice for him because I indeed know of his worthiness, of his untiring service of others and of his constant goodness. My friend has reaffirmed my belief in the Roman Priesthood and now stands before me as a friend and Priest. This quiet church symbolizes the quiet, regulated day-to-day living out of his commitment to service of others, when the joys and festive moments give way to the long days of routine, loneliness, and quiet inner peace.

## SOLIDARITY WITH THE ABSOLUTE

I am confident that there is an underlying solidarity with the Absolute that will make itself manifest if I allow it to do so. The last four weeks have taught me an immensity of things: the inner peace and harmony of my solitude here each day, the exhausting yet uplifting feeling of having done a good job, the realization that I had significantly contributed to another man's cause for celebration, the awareness that I had labored and prayed myself to a peaking experience, that I had opened up to the possibility of experiencing God and other people in love, friendship and thanksgiving.

## ON THE GREYHOUND BUS NEAR INDIANAPOLIS, INDIANA

This bus trip is long and gruelling. The night is stormy and lightning sometimes illuminates the fields and rows of houses along the road. I sit here counting to ten over and over again, slowly calming my mind and emotions, counting, and gradually forming a prayer with my being: " *Jesus!*"

## AT MY SISTER'S HOME: FORT RECOVERY, OHIO

I think that for the first time in my life I am understanding what married life is all about and what a celibate life is all about. I am learning too that I must stand on my own convictions, that no other human being must absorb all my attention and energy. This means not that I love less those whom I know already but that I must love without dependencies, without attachments, that I must love all people equally.

## THE SAME THING ON MY MIND

Still I awake every day with the decision of monasticism before me and go to bed at night with the same thing on my mind.


## MY BEST TEACHERS

My Mother and my Father are my best teachers about a true spirit of Christian poverty.


## PRIMROSE STREET & KESSLER BOULEVARD

Quickly fall
the Autumn leaves
reminders of
the time that flees
leaving here
the same old man
yet always someone new


## ONLY GOD KNOWS

Only God knows what will happen to me and He is keeping it a big secret.


## AN INTEGRATED WHOLE

I must not establish polarities and set up antitheses.  I must see all things as valid parts of an integrated whole.

## SUNRISE IN THE PENNSYLVANIA MOUNTAINS

God, what a gift!
This glorious sunrise in the Pennsylvania Mountains.
Now a fiery sphere
cushioned by clouds,
mist-draped hills and the Morning Star.
What more to long for?

Sleep wishes to overcome
me, overcome by the beauty.
Both shall win me over.


## A DECISION

I am advised to make a decision before the end of 1973.  I am afraid and
apprehensive.


## TO SIT ONCE MORE IN JOURNAL SQUARE

Ah yes,
to sit once more in Journal Square
and to watch and listen for
Life's footstep-sound
upon the littered ground.
Quickly cross: the "WALK" won't "WAIT"
the traffic mounts around.

Below rattles rumble train
from Newark at minute mark
for a moment here to stop
then on to

New York City across the River
sky-filled yet silently seen
and me here at 3:15
and now it's almost 4.

# NEW YORK CITY GLEAMING

I lift the shade, peek through the blinds
across the street and farther East to see
New York City gleaming
cast bronze-like by November sunset

Nightly lights now beaming
past time-long-gone bridges suspended

I think on days when just a boy
so mystified by that city
and realize though both have grown
the magic is remaining


# GOD SPEAKS

God speaks through the unexpected.


# GOD WILL LEAD ME

There is so much that is beyond me, things hidden from my understanding, things out of my range of control, things that humiliate me, make me dependent, things that simply bewilder me. Yet I am optimistic and deep within believe that God will lead me to the fulness of peace to which he called me long ago.

## SAINT PATRICK'S CATHEDRAL

God would have it that
I be here once again.
A return to beauty sometimes
seen as such and
other times not so
by me in the past.
Sometimes immense
and sometimes small it is
still the same here.

## WITH HEART GROWN STRONG

This morning, while the clock tower chimed 10:00 A.M., I left for New York
City. I knew that I had to go there primarily for one reason, to go to confession
in the city that is so symbolic of my life, to be able to leave the past behind in
this very graphic way. I went to confession and celebrated my "First Eucharist"
at Saint Patrick's Cathedral. Many times I have been there and with many
different attitudes and emotions. Today I came as a sinner, all too aware of my
regrettable condition and lofty hopes. I left a healed man, with heart grown
strong and desires directed to one end, serving God as a monk.

## POEM TO THE SPIRITUAL MASTER

Father, Master of Manliness and wisdom,
your virtue, your reknown, your well-known goodness
drew me to your side when I was
but a wayfarer and so much in need
of aid. I stuttered words tacitly,
knowing of your grace,
and fumbled miserably for the ways
to describe my wretched state.

*"Father, I have come to drink of your*
*cup of Wisdom,"* I muttered,
wondering how the words got through
my dry and tightened throat.

You eased my pain with the Word,
and warmed me with your warmth,
and listened carefully to my words
which added not to much.

You dispelled quickly my gnawing doubts
and restored my heart in Peace.

And so one visit grew to two and
tripled ten times more, and never ever
did I tire of knocking at your door.
Sometimes I came a penitent
and other times a friend,
but always when I left your room,
I left a better man.

When last we saw, you blessed my days,
and sent me on my way. *"Blend the now
with the Eternal Now. Bring meaning to
people's lives. Be at Peace."* Since
that time I've travelled wide and it seems
that I've greatly grown. There were times
when I lost your words and found
only anguish. More clearly now I
hear your words, more dearly they are cherished.


## TO MY LADY OF SORROWS

I love you, my Lady, in many ways,
for your presence in me,
as Mercy's Queen and Purity,
as Wisdom's Resting Place.

Yet most dearly do you I love,
as Lady Most Sorrowful,
with wistful stance and guarded glance,
with pale and saddened face.

Not to pain do I pledge my love,
rather to your beauty,
wrought by strain and a mother's love,
loss and dreadful anguish.

Your seven swords pierce my eyes,
and pierce my memory dulled,
and bring to life in a grace-filled way,
the old Simeon's saying.

The Nightly Flight, the Loss of the Loved,
the torturous Calvary Way,
stabbed at your heart and tore at your soul,
and yet you continued on.

You stood at His feet as He hung on the Cross,
and held Him dead in your arms,
and defying all limits of your manly love,
you sealed Him in His tomb.

My love, my Lady, it makes me cry,
so frail and sinfully hollow,
yet I give it to you tearfully,
to ease your pain and sorrow.


## TO THOMAS MERTON

I set a fire
reminder of you
alive no longer
but in my heart
and the hearth-fire
burns bright as
the memory that glows - You!

## DIACONATE: A REMINISCENCE

I see you clear on Abbey stones
as Evening's sun sets.

We pass our thoughts in whispered words,
we stop, we hush,
to let penetrate the joys of the day
and the uncounted sorrows to come.

Barely dare I speak
my deep-most sentiments, lest the
sun go down without eye's good-bye,
lest you spy the tear gathered
in my eye and laugh away
my sadness.


## NATIVITY

crating wood splinters
prick my fingers
fashioning
shipping-box boards
into
Christmas stable

little used wood
forms baby's crib
and rusty bent nails
with shattered slats
make
hay-loft rails
and
angel's stand

# HYMN TO SNOW

I stay my prayer
forgive me, Lord
I stop to watch
the snow
on furrowed ground
and falling down
and melting
on my nose

And pardon, Lord
if I pass
from lofty thoughts
in your praise
to mind's
silence's sweet
content

Great Giver's gift
it surely is
and plentiful
indeed

for fun and
play and
poetry
and just
to stand
and gaze


# I HOLD MY BREATH

I hold my breath at the thought of Christ.
I must learn to grow in his love.

# HYMN OF THE THREE KINGS

I kneel in adoration to my King,
not of earthly riches.
Nay, rather Lord of Simpleness,
and I of temporal treasures.

I kneel in adoration to my Sage,
not of worldly learning.
Nay, rather Lord of Wisdom Great,
and I of reason's wranglings.

I kneel in adoration to my Master,
not of material forces.
Nay, rather Lord of Clemency,
and I of stately statutes.


# I AM GOING AWAY

I am going away
you will perhaps
look for me
and perhaps you
may not find me

Where I am going
you cannot come
I go not
because I am
good
but for what
must be done

## ZEN POVERTY

With two dollars in my pocket
and six new books on *Zen*
I ponder which to buy and go home empty handed laughing.


## SEE HOW THEY LOVE PECK

See how they love-peck
these two sparrows
not knowing that a blue-jay watches.


## TAKE THE TIME

Take the time it's yours
and do with it what you will
there are no boundaries to your freedom
and take the chance
to break away from that

old self-reliance
give a care to another's need
to take you by the hand


## RESPLENDENT THE MIST

Resplendent the mist
the morning's slumber
ends awakens the
day tomorrow is
now leaving behind
its memories in hours
already past

# FILL MY MIND WITH THOUGHTS OF LOVE

Fill my mind with thoughts of love
from my heart banish all selfishness
Make of me a giving man
choosing good above all else


# ENDLESSLY CHANT I

Endlessly chant I
beneath the stars
*"I believe in love,"*
seeking no other to sway,
only myself to prove.


# LINES UPON RECEIVING A PACKET
# OF PHOTOGRAPHS

Ah, what debt we owe to science
whose produced images
more clearly depict
what mind
has lost long ago and
struggles anew to remember


# NOW THAT YOU ARE GONE

Do you think that you can so easily be forgotten
Now that time and distance separate us
And Seasons change and Holidays pass?
Much more than need in Friendship is begotten.
And time and distance affect not closeness.
And Nature and festivity gauge that which lasts.

No picture nor token need I
To be reminded of you, my friend.
The wind, the trees secretly whisper your name.
As our once conversation is now ended.
Will not our strong bond stay the same?

## LEAVING

Vigils - packing - Lauds - packing
Mass - packing - waiting - leaving.

## LIFE MOMENTS

The ritualization of significant life moments.
Everywhere - always

## SUN LOW AT OLDENBURG

Spires and trees splinter the sun
windows aglow as if a fire raged inside

## ONE MONK ONCE WROTE WORTHY WORDS

One monk once wrote worthy words
holding them as holy

preaching them so boldly
and losing all his friends

# RAIN

clear and moon-full sky
has given way
to rain


# THE MOON

I was sad
at the passing
of time
Until
I saw
the . . . moon.


# SILENCE

For every statement
there is made
a deeper silence
pervades


# NO THING

Nobody owes a thing to anyone;
No one responds by wanting.

## SHATTERED SLEEP

sleep shattered by
lights and loud talk

a happy girl with a new baby-doll
sings sweetly in my ear and giggles
at my antics


## GOD AND FRIENDSHIP

Lord, show me the way
to do your will.  I thank you
for friendship!


## I SAW A TULIP TREE

I saw a tulip tree
and stopped to ask
if it were such,
thinking it to be
a dogwood.


## ON READING KEATS

strange not that I be
reading Keats before going
to Conyers. *"I think I think
too much,"* I say, and
not so unlike him.

# I CHANCED UPON A HERMIT'S HUT

I chanced upon
a hermit's hut
while walking
the woods
of Conyers


# THE UNSEEN GOD

Seeing the river's movements
reflected in a web
I pondered the workings
of the unseen God


# HELL

Hell is a hollow existence.
It holds you fast-chained
to the horrors of your past
and flings you headway
into the future's confusions.


# BITTERSWEET THE MEMORY

it's fine
such finality
which made him uneasy
bittersweet the memory
you are too far away

# A SOURCE OF CONSTANCY

Let us share our readings
and our doings
And forever let us be
to each a source of constancy
In love and hope and living


# BEAUTY TOO BEAUTIFUL TO BE REAL

Beauty too beautiful to be real
I had never seen before
deer tracks in the clay
nor steam rising above the lake
the way it rose today

# AMETHYST HOUR

## I.

To string strains of the imagination
mind's musicians tuned.
Flutes blew color accompaniments,
to the humming of the sparrows.
Peacock fans cooled the thought—
swans serenely gliding,
eased along by melodies deep,
moos of ancient cows grazing,
memories lingering, languishing,
to wistful aquatic lutes,
teased silent by the memories,
diasporatic doubts drew still.
Mocked away by celestes in play,
detachment disappeared,
loosing locks left in its wake,
sensations long, too long, impounded.

## II.

In the quake of sudden excitation,
configurations pranced:
chimeras of friendship in pantomime,
iris shafts in "flag-tag" games with
crocus deeds and words now spoke
by marigold magicians,
floral images prickly and perfumed,
cartwheels of wizard hues descending,
alighting on lady spider's mat,
web of continuities,
pleasure's spindle strung and smooth,
miniature mandalas of moments past,
regained, rewrought in silvery threads,
resplendent strands of joy,
and love and constancy reborn,
time-tried wires of wonderment.

III.

To heart rush through harp-hung willows,
reed symphonies arose.
Mandarin courtesans cleared the air,
wielding antic lyres leafy and long.
By emotions moved and *tambura* taps,
mind's eye turned to the sun.
Obeisant caught at the moment's heights,
Passion splashed across the sky.  In
incessant chants of charring light
the fiery orb broke through,
great orient groom from his chamber come,
burst of mind and bathed in bliss,
robed in rows of ruddy splendor,
glad champions rejoicing,
to the mad musifications dancing,
and slipping away at the amethyst hour.

IV.

*"Truth of all these beautiful lies,"*
the monk-poet writes.
Yes, lies no more than fleeting joys,
awareness, not of malice born,
but by Beauty begot and sadly
brought to rest too long
on things that pass:  Truth thus
mistrued by impermanence.
These are the deceivers:  the 'gems and
the jewels' that adorn the world,
players of musicales in the mind,
makers of flirtation with the senses.
Writ by the poet as "new world inaugurated,"
'tis none but the meet
of Beauty and man in the fuschia time
of all complexities marvelously undone.

## THE SQUARES . . .

The squares, the Bohemes,
the beats, the folks,
the rocks, the hips,
the yips, the freaks,
the squares . . .


## *PROSPEXUS* FOR A POEM ABOUT SAINT JOHN'S CHURCH: INDIANAPOLIS, INDIANA

Your arched aisles wooed
me near, a place of
peaceful rest amidst
my struggles


## THE MOCKING BIRDS

The mocking birds
chatter mocking
the cold
for its chilliness
call all
to warm times


## LIFE-FORCE: YOUR LOVE THAT GLOWS

I am so obsessed with your presence
that the morning sun does not blind
me to it, with its red and fiery light.
More beautiful even than this is your
love that glows.

# IN THE DIRE HOUR OF DEJECTION

In the dire hour of dejection
turn your heart to the
memory of love—therein is
your consolation.


# PLANTHOUSE:  HOLY SPIRIT ABBEY

We need
sort of
a continual mist.


# I HEAR IT

The relentless pounding
of your presence,
I hear it in the cloister,
I hear it in the woods,
The impassioned pleading
of love,
The hope of consolation.


# THE SAINTLY *THÉRÈSE*-IAN CHURCH MOUSE

The saintly *Thérèse*-ian church mouse
bit the Trappist cheese,
got caught in a trap of love,
and never will regret it.

## CENSORIOUS TOUCHINESS

censorious touchiness
tepidity


## GOOD FRIDAY: VIGILS

White rows of monks,
across the choir,
asleep:
*"Can you not watch with
Me one hour?"*


## HOLY SATURDAY: A WALK

They piped Him
a tune,
the sad tune
of Death.

They piped it
in the woods
they piped it
in the cloister.

They piped Him
a tune,
the sad tune
of death.

# ON THE CITY BUS: INDIANAPOLIS, INDIANA

49x4426
the auto of care
got me there
in time


# ON THE GREYHOUND BUS: EFFINGHAM, ILLINOIS

Buster rider Merton reader
the coach is on its way
scribble scriber hour eater
your funny tales relate:
pleaser feeder fountain stop
ice upon my lap
pass the joint
the black man's drunk
the driver's not around


# REASONINGS DEMAND

Reasonings demand
out of
foolish words.

From gentleness's
countenance
a faint smile
radiates the coldness.

The rain-studded
window
opens out to clouds
and the travel call
is heard.

Affections melt and merge.

A song of
poignant lyric
answers to the mood.

Alternatives of care
—never to be arrived at.

Tomorrow maybe
there will be
a dawn.


# THE CRUCIFIX OF SANTA FE

LUKE 23:42

*Bultos Cristos* on the dark wall suspended
my mind on gift wood *reredos*
and bejeweled *Conquistadors*

I turn to find your glass-eyed
gaze and human hair
scrutinizing wellspring of unending kindness
whispering words of love to this wanderer

And a friend takes my hand along the way
away to other images waiting to remind
this failing heart of You


# SADNESS SHATTERED

a tear hung from my eye
a rainbow spectrum
burst in
and in a glimpse
my sadness shattered

.

## PAYSON, ARIZONA

moon and star
and twilight


## THIS HARMONY OF PEACE

guitar strings strummed
in love and
choruses of fun rising
voices of girls
and little boys and
men and women joining
what is love if not
this harmony of peace?


## ON THE TRAIN IN L.A.

Bring the bags quickly we plead
trains never wait for human affection
to be given and shared yet now
I'm here and still sitting still
but nervously and what will it
all bring


## JET STREAM: L.A.

Jet stream in crescent curve
Griffith Park sunset a palm tree
a hazy distant line of clouded hills
L.A. traffic on the side streets
perimetered by tracks of passenger
trains on the move.

From a porch a woman waves sadly
and young girls gladly
and a car driver gives the finger.
It is gorgeous but there is
goodness elsewhere.
A thousand questions
so suddenly answered.
The jeweled kingdom of Pasadena
purple opulence defining lights.

## FLAGSTAFF, ARIZONA

The mountains,
pine-covered,
fill the vista.

## NEARING LAGUNA, NEW MEXICO

A jack-rabbit in the desert.
Get about a decision now.
This land is imbued
with the spirit of the Lord.

## *SANGRÉ DE CRISTO* MOUNTAINS
IN THE DISTANCE

I remember sitting for hours
in the middle of a field
in silent communion
with a sunflower.

# SUNFLOWER MEMORY

sunflower once seen
in a South Bend field
found in memory
in the desert of New Mexico


# RURAL EVENING RUGGED TERRAIN

Colorado Rockies sunshine's bright
but I keep the shade up to take
in the scenery.
Streams and caverns falling rocks
rural evening rugged terrain
pioneered by me tonight.


# *PURGATORRE* RIVER

Double-breasted mountains
firm forms heaved above the flatland sleek
distant trails of ranges maiden sentinels
a drape of purple hue provocative enough
to catch my eye and keep it, and me,
a captive gazer
a jet streams above you
I am jealous of its rapacious viewpoint

The Colorado sun sets
across the plains
hemmed by hedges of stone
rimmed, wreathed by rugged ravines
and the *yucca* grows here too
rivulets cool the eyes red from the sun
mistaken for a cloud another mountain top
(and he crossed me on the forehead)
A bombast of colors as I close my eyes. . .

# DIVINE IMPOSITION

Divine imposition:
sacred affliction of something
indefinable a mandate to be
nothing other than great in
selflessness denials evoked
from a questioning heart
unrequited doubts abound.


# NEAR FRENCH LICK, INDIANA

A rainy day in Southern Indiana;
the pelting against the windshield.


# SOUTHERN INDIANA, ENROUTE TO INDIANAPOLIS

A stormy ride through mist
and hazy hills.


# HOME #1

Night—quiet rest at home.  Amen.


# THE DEATH OF RELATIONSHIPS

The death of relationships,
come let us lament,
and maybe even laugh
away the sorrow,
for tomorrow
we will meet anew.

# THE COSMOS

Singing songs
of
years gone by,
laughing away the hours
with a beer
in  hand
and a guitar.
When?
Where?
Why?
I was born
to make time
to the Cosmos.


## *MAHABODHISATTVA #1*

He came along in robes of gold
a fortune worth of

Speech
he subdued
few and well-chosen symphonies
of wisdom
spewed along the way
Teachings
by way of inaction

Aggregates
teased flesh and reasoning
taut fibers of feeling and thought

Aggregates
teased flesh and reasoning
taunt fibers of emotive power
congruities of time past and moments

yet to come
he walked along

A child he caressed along the way
holding it in his arms

He left her weeping crystals
clear aggregates released
by a caressing hand
gently pressed against her eyes

Aggregates of cognition
feelings and perceptions interwoven
he strode the road
a wicker hat to shade him
from a fame too great for comfort

He left her weeping crystals
clear aggregates released by a
gentle hand gently placed
across her pallid cheek

He left, she wept crystal tears
beads of aspiration
and pressed a hand to the cheek
that took his gentle touch
in the flickering of a wish
the aggregates
dissolved


## GRAY SKIES OF RESTFULNESS

gray skies of restfulness
a tranquil heart greets the day
a sense of correctness in the morning

# PART TWO:  MONASTIC POEMS

1974 - 1995

# POSTULANCY AND NOVITIATE

## JUNE 29, 1974 - NOVEMBER 28, 1976

## HOME #2

The "bingo marker"
sun
welcomes
me
home!


## DEEPER THAN THE RECESSES

Deeper than the recesses
explored
by any former
lover
are the depths
I
will
lay open
to the gaze
of the future.


## "THE DISPARITY OF DREAMS"

*"The Disparity of Dreams,"*
that is what she called
our liaison,
after it started to crumble.

## MAHABODHISATTVA #2

He left she wept crystal beads
tears of sweet affliction
and pressed a hand to the cheek
that took his gentle kiss.

He wept she left a golden chain
around his languished heart.
He walked beneath the *ginkgo* trees
and caressed the clamoring children.


## BABY *RICHELIEU'S* DEMISE

*"Life is hell when you are old and lonely,"* said the
homosexual
on TV.

*"Life is a brick,"* said the girl in the movie last
night.
For her there were no preliminaries last night.  He
got himself
off on her last night without waiting.

*"Life is a brick!"*  Fake liaisons, fading
orgasms, treaties
of deceit.

*"We cannot feel responsible for her suicide, but
we must ask if
we loved her enough,"* said the priest at her
Funeral Mass last
week.

Who remembers all the lost ones too afraid to cry
for help?
Who remembers all the shopping-bag ladies living
just on the
edges of life?  Sordid, raped, robbed shopping-bag
ladies?

Or those just too afraid to let go of their
nightmare existences?
Controlled, insecure, unapproved, unhealthy,
unclean, unhappy?

Full of verbal disavowals and evasions from the
Law, who cares for
them?

The girls played like new records by their
boyfriends, who remembers
them?  Girls so anxious, so desperate to
experience life's nakedness
with another, to touch someone just once beyond
the physical, beyond
the usual devastation of their souls:  *"Hold me
tight and tell me
who I am!"*  *"Who are you?"* she asks.  His
actions tell her who.
*"Am I here?"* she begs for something permanent.
*"Where am I?"* she asks
in melancholy disembodiment.  So lonesome
himself for something lasting,
something real, he still slams her with his needs
and then says
*"Get off my back!"*

## CANDLELIGHT AND COUNTER-LITURGIES #1

Candlelight—counter liturgies:
the newspaper crumpled as you pretended to
interest
and stared right through the words you didn't
read
refusing to look me in the eyes.

*"How many nights can we spend like this?"*
How many nights, I remember, we rumpled
the sheets, not caring, refusing all distractions
of wind and sound and any other's touches.


## CANDLELIGHT AND COUNTER-LITURGIES #2

*"PLEASE LOVE ME,"* the persistent plea of
broken humanity.

*"YOU CAN'T DEMAND AFFECTION,"* comes
the reply from life.

*"We went to a (love it or leave it) party for a draft
resister."*

*"Did you love it or leave it?"* I demanded and
slammed the door, nearly shattering the transom
glass.

*"Stop apologizing for living,"* I preach to myself,
and don't
believe my words.

The candlelight flickers through double brandies
and peach
daiquiris. Though I choose Seagrams I feel like
my head is in
a Singapore sling with a Black Russian cast.
*"Bloody Mary,
how long can this go on?"* *"Please pass the
coke."*

## ASTROLOGICAL FANCIES

Astrological fancies
from
a
hidden source
of wonder.
It is Fall!


## SUCH AS THE CRAZY MAN IN *ZEN*

Such as the crazy man in *Zen,*
he stalks the winter woods in barefeet
and warms you with his welcome
to a rickety 'reclusion' just two doors
down from the barnyard.


## VALENTINE IN *ANNO DOMINI*

Who could deny his good looks?  Who could like his feelings?

*"You sure get around for a choir boy,"* said the now nameless gay from
Germany.  Four former seminarians outstanding in liturgy and the arts, music
and disenchantment, entertained with champagne and cheese omelets for
breakfast.  Four former Catholics had no need for a fast.  They served tea in high
fashion on cane-back chairs on the sun porch, just beyond the living room of red
trimmed in white.  Upstairs a needlepoint chair and a double bed with a floral-
patterned bedspread in one room.

I stayed in a guest room with books on *Zen*, WALK ON! by Christmas
Humphreys.  The others had come just for the morning.  And beneath it all a
pervasive, jealous suspicion.  How terrible loneliness is!

# WHEN THE MOON HUNG A LANTERN IN THE TREES

With satin-finished fingernails
she lifted the lattice-shade
and peered beyond the book she read
looking for her lover.

He came from the North when the moon hung
a lantern in the trees
through porticos of blue and pools of jade
hushed to her room by maidens in gauze.

She said she read the *TAO* OF LOVE
and found him in each rhyme
he pressed her with his kiss
and caressed her sequined eyes.

He melted to the candle
of her warm embrace,
by her own mouth restrained
lest his gasps be heard.

They slept in the silks
of their warm wet night
as courtesans peeked
to check their harm.

The cooling of the breeze warned
of the coming of the morn
and frightfully she remembered
the nearness of their doom.

He fled with the moon to the
regions of the North,
as she entered the chamber
of her stirring Lord.

He fled with the moon to the
regions of the North,
a promise to return
his last whispered words.

## "LADY *CHARTREUSE*"

She paints her face in chartreuse
the fairy queen of night
and walks and stalks the hallways
of Anastomon
decrying her fate and lately jeering
down the walkways of *Prades.*

He lays her open along the East Coast
of Cyanosis
rips wide her disguise
forces her to swallow
her pride
rapes her mind
and leaves her to self-pity.

The *"Chartreuse Lady"* wakes
in pain and carries on no more
*"Sometimes,"* she says, *"it hurts
too much to live."*


## "JEAN JESTER"

*"Jean-Jester"* your themes I'll sing
with zither strings rightly tuned to laughter
and scatter pepper in the air
to see what follows after

Planets through the popcorn trees
and clowns in the muffins
music notes on your tie
and wizards in the attic
gaslights in the sky
and a moon that beams a smile
talking Turkish to the moos
and sailboats in the soup dish

*"Jean-Jester"* your world I'll sing
in melodious rings of children's chatter
and ponder puns in nursery rhymes
to see which is the dafter

Riffs of Chopin in the night and zany hats of
learning a wig of wit and cheeks of red
moiré tufts and purple puffs

dancing saffrons in the air
slippery slides of tournaments
figures in the making

*"Jean-Jester"* your themes I'll sing
with merry admiration


## LOVE YOURSELF

Love yourself
as others
love you!

After you've had
a couple of years
of lonely nights
you begin
to see
where love really is.

# EACH ONE CONTINUES TO TEACH ME

Each one continues
to teach me
something.

Each one has had
a different experience
of God.

Each one whispers
different words
to
the Lord.


# BLISS OR SORROW

An invitation to her room.
How I had often wondered
what would usher forth
from my lover's womb:
would it be bliss or
sorrow in human form?


# ROOM BLESSING

Redoing the *Zen* stole
*Ryokan's* hut is of cinder block
grass shoots sprout in vases
window glass leaves encase
and rain cleans the slate
roof in tricklets.

## MAY

Mass
visit in sacristy
breakfast
talk
tour
rest
supper on balcony
apples
cheese
cookies
wine
soda
hike
hermitage
rabbits
sun
creek
clay
camera
deer leaps
electric wires
rest


## THERE IS ALWAYS SOMETHING TRAGIC

There is always something
slightly tragic
in your smile.
The lesser
man
is blessed
by the greater.
Prior to
and beyond all teaching
a compassionate
heart
guides
your way.

# WHISPERJET SONG

We are never good at "goodbyes";
the last few hours we are irritable.
You get silent, withdrawn, pensive.
I seem to cling to each moment,
only knowing that it will pass.
There have been waves on dusty roads,
and half-smiles in bus stations,
and quiet "be well's" in airports,
all with awkward gesture,
knowing that it's time to go,
but always hoping for the next time.


# DEAR *KIERKEGAARD*

Open disclosures. . .
just one night with
you, if only. . .

Dear Kierkegaard,
will you allow me
to call this. . .
"the teleological
suspension of
the ethical"?


# ST. MARY'S SEMINARY:  RECOLLECTIONS

Black the birds
in motionless glide
the fields open wide
to the sunset
the stillness speaks
for us—a return to
calm and three
return home
in twilight

# RECOLLECTION OF FIRST WALK

chianti wine—apples—cheese
yellow jersey—pine trees
near the vineyard


# YAO-ENG

The shaking of the branch
as the bird flew
*Yao-eng*
amongst the jade carved
*Kuan-yins*
paper fans and flowers


# CRICKET DRILL ALONG THE WALK

cricket drill along the walk
cadence the night
fade through the trees day
take with you all distinctions
darkness calm my tempest deep
beckon come the rest of whispers

with silent stars
to soothe my fears until tomorrow
cadence the night crickets
drill along the walkways
escort the light
beyond the cloister
through the trees
disburse all distinctions
cricket drill along the walk
cadence the night

# THE TURTLE AND THE LIZARD

Hey!  Speak to me
mischievous guests
in the cloister
as you distract me from
my book.


# REPOSE RESTLESS SUN

The clouds move as persons through the day
there is a coming together and a parting
a momentary breeze
a moon that rises pale yet peaceful
sway of the branch at the flight
of the evening swallows

Recline this moment you are here now
these realities are conceived
they are dreams dreamt most deeply
hopes whispered aloud and received
thoughts recast in wonderment
they are come to be
joys do rise to truth

Be gone now to distant destinations
there is one who keeps you near
reflect upon the sands and waves
these joys do not end but nurture
tomorrow's gladness
in intimacies too deep for words
too secret for retelling
the passing is what lasts
what is over has not yet begun
it waits in the distant days
it calls for greater caring

To give up is to gain more than ever owned
to receive more than ever reasoned
such simple joys in silent times

they cannot stay but do remain
in silent recollection

To carry lightly the burden of concern
to laugh when feeling lonely
to delight in others when wanting
to be together
to thank for what is taken

Visit me with gladness happy friend
find in me your mirror
the echo is the answer to our
common hesitation
it is thankful and sublime
it cares for you

Repose restless sun and weary
too much too soon the day brings
and takes before the awakening
it is no dream


## NO SCHOOL BOOK *ZEN*

Transplanting tomatoes
and reading
the PLATFORM *SUTRA*
of *Hui-neng*
I get a glimpse
of Nature
as it is.


## SILENCE

Rust hue moth
rests
on leaded glass.

# A SCHOOL BOY'S DREAM

A school boy's dream:

With a castration anxiety
to match his paranoia
he parades around the school
with a machete in his hand
and keeps asking: *"Is
my penis prodigious?"*

A school boy's dream.


# NIGHT LIGHTS

orange light and moon-shape
a candle and
a tree-lamp
satellites of yellow sparkle
enchanting flits in blackness
here and there and gone
to blackened brightness away
pacing past the window


# WHAT WOULD *ABBÉ DE RANCÉ* SAY?!!!

X is running around
in a red, white, and black
Philadelphia Flyers
jersey
yellow fluorescent
coveralls
and a
pith helmet. . .

What would *Abbé
de Rancé* say?!!!

He looks
like
something
from
Godspel.

What would *Abbé*
*de Rancé* say?!!!


## PASSING OVER TO THE OTHER SIDE

the old lutenist
somewhere in the
mountains plays
a young girl sings
could it be you too
leave to chase
October mists?


## BROTHER

Hard rain concerts
and quiet walks.  Peace-filled silences
and times of hope.  Blessings and an
understanding heart:  You!

## APOTHEOSIS

Anything I compose involves all whom I know and love. My verse is the mystery of my existence made transparent. In this poem I am attempting to construct a dialogue with Jesus, attempting to get the feelings out, feelings of yesterday brought to the present in packed images and gradually reduced word patterns which bespeak an inner peace, the silent peace of love.

Ὅτε οὖν ἠρίστησαν λέγει τῷ Σίμωνι Πέτρῳ ὁ Ἰη-
σοῦς· Σίμων Ἰωάννου, ἀγαπᾷς με πλέον τούτων; λέγει
αὐτῷ· ναί κύριε, σὺ οἶδας ὅτι φιλῶ σε. λέγει αὐτῷ· βόσκε τὰ ἀρνία μου. λέγει αὐτῷ πάλιν δεύτερον· Σίμων
Ἰωάννου, ἀγαπᾷς με; λέγει αὐτῷ· ναί κύριε, σὺ οἶδας ὅτι
φιλῶ σε. λέγει αὐτῷ· ποίμαινε τὰ πρόβατά μου. λέγει αὐτῷ τὸ τρίτον· Σίμων Ἰωάννου, φιλεῖς με; ἐλυπήθη
ὁ Πέτρος ὅτι εἶπεν αὐτῷ τὸ τρίτον· φιλεῖς με; καὶ λέγει αὐτῷ· κύριε, πάντα σὺ οἶδας, σὺ γινώσκεις ὅτι φιλῶ
σε. λέγει αὐτῷ [ὁ Ἰησοῦς]· βόσκε τὰ πρόβατά μου.

GOSPEL OF JOHN 21:15-17

". . . caro salutis est cardo."

Tertullian, DE RESURRECTIONE CARNIS 8

"O let me think it is not quite in vain
To sigh out sonnets to the midnight air!"

John Keats, TO HOPE, 27-28

104

I.
You will be called forth from flesh.
You will be born in flesh and live
in flesh.  You will suffer in flesh and
die in flesh.  Because of flesh you will
live and suffer and die in flesh.

Do you love me?
You know that I love you.
Your flesh is your salvation!

You will be born in half and you
will never heal.  You will be born
and you will live in separation from yourself
and you will die in separation from yourself.
Do you love me?
Lord, you know already that I love you.
Without your flesh you cannot be saved!

You will be called forth from nature.
You will be given more than nature naturally
gives.  You will be born and you will live
and you will suffer from what nature gives.
And you will die in separation from yourself.

Do you truly love me?
Lord, you know all things.  You know that I love
you more than any other whom I
love and I know that you love me.
Through your flesh you will be saved.  Come to me!

II.
Amidst the travail of a restless age
the cyclic fish encompassed
on a nameless ferial made blest
by symbols still laid hidden
the one wrapped in promise.

Brought forth in love and expectation
on the eastern coast of Cyanosis
solemn and slow in movement
a boy to bear his added pain
a joy of vast fulfillment.

105

The pain of one in labor prayed in
valleys of color nearest death
awake and anxious to give herself
in love and blood and motherhood
a boy an answer to her prayers.

Son of one from across the sea
born the son of a Kaiser's knight
the one who came to learn the language
of a new distant shore who taught
tales of castles on the Rhine

They met she of magnanimous eyes
a modesty never forgotten and
he of simple village life where feasts
once were commemorated with banners
and outdoor shrines of wood.

A jewel set the opulence of love
yet after the first-born a tragedy
arose Satan with a knife changed
their lives febrile episodes in the dark
the new-born boy is blue.

Unsettle the songs of youth
unrecognizable forms in the night
black the night beginning they would
sign documents of promise if he should die
not to blame the doctors there must be light.

III.
You will not see the stars until the sun
goes down. You will not see in the darkness
until the lights go out. When you awake
you will realize what has happened to you.
It is then you will see the heavens opened.

IV.
The moon began to speak of peace
a repose not to be disturbed by hard
and ordinary ways the depths of a path
to be explored in weariness
purging the inner entanglements

ultimately a mysterious thing an
incomprehensible gift it was to be
the painful purification of a love
that endures the deepest love
never diminished
the pain but an early stage
to that which is never lost when
given to another early lessons in
dying the first tasting of something
so vast and pure and good
as never to be satisfied again.

V.

Allow yourself not to ask the question, *"What
does it mean?"* All men are born with defective
hearts. You will be made qualified to speak
about my heart from your heart. Take my love
and turn it deep within.

You will come to see that it is the crying
of all men. Each instant of your life I am
with you. It is I in each person you meet
in each new day you greet in each breath
in each hope in the isolation of your lonely
nights.

VI.

In chrism oil unbeknownst it began and grew
sickly and sad on the day of Reception until the next
when accompanied by a knight now strange I took you
to my soul as *"first time Guest"* unknowing
and chrism poured on a head that hurt a slap
too symbolic to be understood at the time it was
given a call to give and not yet attained but in a new
way discovered unresolved conflicts of care and
misdirected love the invalidity of circumstances ordered
and solemn beyond measure endured in lack of cognizance.

At every stage required to wait resistance in disguise
conflicting purposes of heart and time and others
an innocent man fearing nothing in the face of accusation
honestly exposing his life to every inquisition
a guiltless man without fear of revelation.

A guilty man thinking all know his guilt
thinking he is detected he will be found out
there can be no two ways of living self-doubts
abound in life given to two masters there is
no adequate explanation it concerns all.

There can be no hiding behind paper and puzzles
the seeds of fear take root with dreaded news and
waiting it is the last reach of the past the twilight
time between what was and what will be there is
no further gift.

VII.
Why Lord do you tease me with life?
Is it to prove my condemnation!
You have closed me in all sides in my
self-wrought vice there is nowhere to turn
nothing of the past is left and there is no future.

My one-time joys torture me fetter me burn me
to my past the goodness of people kills me it is
not their harshness that hurts
there is nothing to be attained
yet in the midst of my apostasy I believe you are present

VIII.
Do you love me more than the others you love?

Lord, you know that I am trying.  There is no peace without
you.

There is no substitute for human affection.  Your flesh will be
your salvation.  Love for you depends on you.

I know Lord. My life is my greatest gift the sum of the
possibilities I seek. It is the power and the means to reach
you. So great the impact of you sustaining my life. But where
is your love?

Look for it only in obscurity. Do not expect it. Find it in the
diffused light of the cloud-covered moon.
Lord, may I always look for you.

IX.
A warm breeze in the night
a walk alone afraid
not knowing not thinking
but feeling all things converging
in the light ahead.

In the distance a lamp dim but
constant against the black surround
knowing it could not be reached
but feeling serenity in its shining
having it ever before me.

By the lake before my feet
I stand thinking of the fleeting world
I find brethren there with faces shining
through little prayer and little sleep
faces the falling stars pushed stars.

Flickering out before the pale moon
slipping over the mountain astrological
fantasies from a hidden source of wonder
all is as it is as I repose in the moment
I love you my Lord my strength my rock
my moon.

X.
Freedom comes from suffering. Do you love me?

Yes, you already know that I love you.

Your freedom is not free. It will come when your loneliness
has turned into solitude, when your emptiness is your poverty
and your fulfillment. Do you love me?

Yes.

Cling to me! Recline with me this night. Nature's luminaries
shine for you in the bosom of the universe. This night I have
begotten you.

Lord, you will not test me beyond my strength. You will never
lead me into harm. I will never be hurt if I cling to you. It is
only my selfishness that keeps me from you. Fill my mind with
thoughts of love and banish from my heart all selfishness.
Strengthen me with your love.

I will not test you beyond your strength. I will give you
a way out. Your flesh will be your salvation. You must search
out the path that will bring you to me forever. You must see
that I am with you in your distress and in your anxious seeking.
Fear not, it is I all along.

Lord, the pains I suffer are not my own. I do not suffer
alone but suffer the common sufferings of all men who search
after you. Your absence blesses us, our pains strengthen us.
Yet I long to feel your presence. Help me not to look back
but forward. I sense peace and unrest at the same time.

XI.
The feeling comes on quickly. It is futility.
All is doomed to webs of human entanglement.
The incessant self-scrutiny goes on, hoping for
a glimmer of hope, agonizing the phantasms of
the past, calling me to the grave.
There is no futurity. Unaccountable encounters with
the past, in people and places unexpected. The
death of relationships. The daily dimension of
affections, closeness and times of separation.

Voices and strings never to be heard again.
I anguish at myself for what I am. There is no
return of affection, only in my mind. It is a
fantasy beyond proportion. I can only laugh
in the face of despair the death of an illusion

more consuming than a faith passed from generations.
It is all a fiction from the past attachments. There
is really no such communication but in wishes. Thank
you for the memories. I laugh at the tears I have shed
over you on lonely nights, not knowing what to do
and hurting, not allowing the desolation to win yet

still not conquered. I cried for you in the night and
wondered what distant road it was that took you. Other
places too are covered with gloom. I see that
it was all so useless. I am not remembered. The
secret thoughts of my heart are left to casual eyes.

Scrawled in blood. Who reads them now?
I want to believe it is not in vain to believe,
that to believe is not empty. You must
be close in your absence. Protect me from myself.
I reach for you.

My last response is silence. There are no words that
speak. Your love to me and mine to you. You are
present in the secrecy of my hurting heart. It is
you, holding me fast in everlasting safety. This
I must believe if I am to live at all.

XII.
You will live in constant warfare with yourself.
But you will win. I will use all who come to you
as my means to you. I will send you all whom you
will need on your way to me. I will give you them
and I will take them for you at the moment
you love them most. And so you will come to see
I am calling you to myself. I am asking you for
myself. I promise myself to you. All I have will
be yours. All you see is mine to give you. The
days of your life will be lengthened. A truce will

be granted to you out of love. You will come to
see that there are no evil ways. Deeper than the
recesses explored by any former lover are the depths
I will lay open to your gaze in the future. You will
be the vortex through which many people will come to me.

It is with my heart that you will experience all
others. You will realize yourself to me. I am near
when you expose yourself to others. I sustain you.
I radiate you and charge you with the power of
my love so that others may be strengthened.

XIII.
Lord, I reach out to you in moments of joy and in
moments of intense trial I curse you. I praise you always.
I love you with my total being. I love you as the love
of my life. But oh that I had a kiss from you as once
I had in other loves. Breathe on me in an unending conversation

of love. I place myself into your hands. I look
for you but see only the host before the face of
our priest, his head, his hands. I hunger for you.
I must tell you so. Forget me not, Lord. There
is nothing left but you. I long for your random

touch, given in a moment's breeze, the warmth
of your kiss and to gaze in silence. But no more
lived than shadows that fade in the face of renewed
surrender. There is no fear now in what is of the
ageless. It is love rediscovered. Apart from you

I have nothing, I am nothing. With you, fullness
of joy in my heart. Expose me to your beauty born
of a new life. Darkness is my immanent movement.
There are no boundaries now, no limitations.
Thank you for the majesty of the moon.

XIV.
Dragonnade night silk satellite night
cocoa-bead moiré-lined night processions
pass through the night moon light
fading light
taking all distinctions
I know you are here!

XV.
White flash through my mind
the clap of thunder overhead
pounding eardrums everlasting
peace nothing to be evaluated
in the fiery execution over the
mountain death and life are one.

Standing on the edge
dropping off the pines
grayness and dampness
below the branches
quiver for an instant

It is night now
in the darkness
I split in half
from head to foot
my sides touch the walls
I do not exist
I am you

I want to scream out the
sanity and insanity are
one Communion it seems

I walk on air above all
the people that are not here
everything is meshed into One
tears come a sunflower
opening whirling spinning
bringing me to the center
I look for the eyes of a
friend and disappear

XVI.
Lord, it is nighting. I can hardly see. Manna of the Jew
Wisdom of the Gnostic, Darkness of the Doctor of darkness,
Grace, God-Giver, I greet you. Absolute and finite somehow
touch this night This is the moment of grace. There is no need
for me to speak. I have only to stand here.

To speak is for sure to lose it. Yet not to speak is betrayal. This
is the food that sustains me. This is the reason for my life. But
this sustenance is not sweet. It is bitterness, pain, death, not of
bloody extinctions, not yet. There is death in not recognizing
myself. I have lost my past and there is

no future. I am dead to the man that I used to be.
Illusive progress none the less complete. I am dead.
This is the cause of my joy. The arrow of death brings
the ointment of life. I rejoice in death the source of life.
If I do not die the gift remains ungiven.

I will die and die again. This is my call to birth.
This is my total submission, my total receiving. I too
have drunk the dregs of loneliness. I too have greeted
the morning sun alone. Yet somewhere a crocus blossoms
fertile with the sweet unction of poetry the beauty of

the desert and useless things. It disdains nothing that
is of love and beauty, the happy swallow that now
has found its nest. Imbue the land of my heart, Lord,
with the same spirit. By whom can I be torn for joy
if not by you, my love, my Lord.

XVII.
If you ever need me I am here.
I love you. I will wipe your tears.
In periods of great loneliness
it is I who am your company.
I feel your aching for me
and I comfort you.
I remember you and promise
to be ever with you.

XVIII.
The relentless pounding of your presence
I hear it in the cloister
I hear it in the woods
the impassioned pleading of love
the hope of consolation.

For all that is dead to me
because of sin and inability
there is still great hope.
You are that hope.

XIX.

For what does it matter to hear the
pounding
if not to succumb to it.
In the dire hour of dejection
turn then your heart to the
memory of love
therein is your consolation.

XX.

Endlessly chant I beneath the stars
*"I believe in love"* weeping for
the ones I've lost longing for
their guidance along my aimless way.
Help me now to be at peace and silent

Lord. Take those I have turned into
the objects of my adoration. Love them
and care for them. They have suffered
from me. Hold them now fast in safety,
in joy without end. Sustain

them as I leave them behind, as I cry
for them in choir, and hope for tomorrow,
that we might meet. For now
no journeys made in haste,
in pain, in fear. We are all held captive
where we are. It is your love.
May a tranquil heart greet tomorrow,
may correctness breathe in the morning air.
Lord, you know all things. You know that
I love you. My ways lead to you. My

existence is of you. My living is for
you. I trust you, Lord, you will not
lead me astray. I need not fear now.
I need not justify my life. It is yours.
Do with it as you will. I

place myself and all those I love upon
the broken paten of our lives in you.

Those I love and will come to love are
all here in you. Jesus in the chalice
the image of myself upside down.

I drink in you as I drink the memories
of love in the past and ponder love
to come. Lord, you will choose for me my
brothers. You will choose for me all those
I will love and will love me.

XXI.
Trappist walls now not so silent
sing then the praises of the God
of the monks who built you
bend to the sound of choruses
that rise higher than your turrets.

Yet stand against an unbelieving age
now that your days are accomplished
and your nights filled with solitaries
heralds now they sing praises louder
than the skeptics can declare the

demise of their calling. Chrismed
corners trumpet peals it seems come
forth from your mitred edges pledges
of continuous prayer for those too poor
to live here. Variances on truth they

seem mute then resonant from lips of
pilgrims passing in the night. Quiet
reed-like melodies unrecognized  soft
tones of processioners who have found
their way home. Sprinkled walls stand

firm.  Incensed vapors pass you too
as escorts.  Well up from your depths
give Glory to the Father and to his
Son and the Spirit within.  Trappist
walls sing their praises sing then the
joy of our hearts the One whose Name

is ever in our mouths.  Burn crossed flames
across the heart of this consecrated
church.  Dance to the music that flows from
below.  Burn into our hearts the memory of
this awesome day on which our lives are

given away.  Hymns and burning oil have
branded you, Day, as perpetual keeper of
our praises and solemn dedication.  A deeper
silence pervades your precincts now more
articulate than the men who die here.

XXII.
Before the solitary light
throwing light against its cold cement
form, the form of one in prayer, whose
hell has churned to acquiescence
knowing that in the closeness there is
you and you in the distance
footsteps in the dark space the
transept tabernacled warmed by the
lamps of prayers of monks in vigils
of their own houring you pass
I pray for understanding.

This night
brought me hoping
praying knowing of your
coming only by faith
to face myself
all is as it should be.

When by the grace of a
waning lamp
I sit choruses sound deep
refined by long compression

into a resonance wordless
almost unheard
like the summer symphonies
of mists
in far-off places
grace and light this night meet.

It is a night when the bell
tower is taller than the moon
full December moon
fearless moon
to scatter light in this room
owl in my ruins
audacious moon unleaded moon on starry night
Trappist incensed moon
cloistered moon.

XXIII.
You have called me forth, Lord
for this night, charring my flesh
long ago with the burning ointments
of illness and separation  You have
called forth from my weary heart

increased prayers and anguished
silences all now harmonized to the
air, to the music and the flames.
And where have I lived all along
but here, in this place, in this

moment here, in this silent audience
of exultation.  Do you hear now as
before, my incensed prayers, my
anguished silences,
eternal redemptive silences?

XXIV.
Do you love me?

Lord of my life, I love you!

XXV.

I will make you eat your words written on a fleshy
scroll the toll of desolation.  And you will come to
see that it is your flesh that is your salvation, after
it has been torn from you piece by piece pain by
pain.  And your love of me will ever grow and I will
take you to my own heart wounded for you and you
will be fulfilled.

XXVI.

My Blackest Brightness, may it be!

# MIND GUARDS AGAINST THE WHITE KNIGHT

He sure carries himself well
while the gendarmes sleep with their weapons loaded
protecting the crown jewels, the wood-be ladder, hot
danish for breakfast and German junk at night
the walls and pines will keep their secrets
when white knight comes
in the future all will be revealed
1976

\*


Resentment
Do you prefer German to Danish?
Take it or leave it!
Making sparks in the dark
hot danish for breakfast, German junk at night
winner of the coupon contest, box-top cereal celebrity
protecting the crown jewels while the gendarmes sleep
with their weapons loaded

\*


When white knight gets here the walls will retain our
secret and the pines will tell it all in silence

\*


He sure carries himself well
dances with the beauties
stays up at night counting his gift money

\*


*"I'm in a hurry,"* he says
*"You always are,"* she says
*"You men are slaves to your own erections."*

\*

The wood-be ladder
the retention wall and pines will keep their secrets
when white knight gets here

\*

Making sparks in the dark
vying for the title of "Pan-Psychic Contender"
Rm 1441
shattered innocence on sand paper
against the night lights
harp tones too proclaim your name
across the sky in C
steeple

\*

He sure carries himself well
while the gendarmes sleep with their weapons loaded
protecting the crown jewels, the wood-be ladder, hot
danish for breakfast and German junk at night
the walls and pines will keep their secrets
when white knight comes
in the future all will be revealed
1976.

## FOR MY CONFESSOR

Thank you for dissipating
the funnel cloud of my storm
with the cool breeze
of your calm.


## A FABLE

This is a fable about Betty Grable
wearing sable under the table
with Clark Gable though neither
were able

transatlantic cable to the brain
underocean lines to the spleen
cosmic rays to the astral nuts


## TRAPPIST ABBEY:  VIGILS

White host moon
on platinum paten roof
Celebrate the day!

# SIMPLE PROFESSION

NOVEMBER 28, 1976 - JUNE, 1982

# DEPARTURE #1

*"He covered them with a cloud."*
        PSALM 104:1-6

*

colored, striped umbrellas
turn like wheels of circus
carts in the rain
twirl like tops
waiting for you.


# DEPARTURE #2

You are here,
seen, not seen,
gone,
seen again,
in a glimpse, then you disappear,
back again,
into oblivion.


# JUMPER RABBIT

Jumper
rabbit
seen
through
the
surveillance
camera.
You!

## FELLOW MYSTERY

Where to begin with the Jesus maybe
you spoke of first day and
travels you went through to find him
here images of your friend
and the Clown in a distant place
faces you said you knew to be the same

Concerts with kazoos and silly things
to divert the hurt in difficult days
and weekends without the ones we
knew better and miss them together
and maybe a tape to tell them
poems & laughter and sometimes disagreement

My over-mind your lack thereof
envious me you sleek and pink and
compensate in writing fables from my memory
you teach the emptiness of words and
the widespread dread of death and God
and loneliness your sincerity unmasks you

Stand white pillar in the moon and
cool out burning. You give it whole I am
not the same for knowing you as we wait
in joy and sometimes tears fellow fools
for the One who somehow holds us all
I am sure you are sure of His whereabouts.

# AND HE IS IN YOURSELF

*"Sed, O Domine, abyffus abyffum invocat: abyffus profundiffime miferiae meae abyffum altiffimae mifericordiae tuae. Quaerens fubfiantiam cui innitar, quam apprehendam, multam ufquam invenis nifi te:...Ubi ergo? In amore. Ibi eft fedes ejus, ibi cubiculum ejus. Amoris affextus in te naturaliter eft. Quem quareris, fi in amore tuo eft, in te eft: fi ibi non eft, in to non eft. Sed quem queris, non quaereres, fi non amares. Habes ergo quem quaeris, & penes te eft..."*

William of St. Thierry, *DE CONTEMPLANDO DEO*

\*

But, O Lord, deep calls unto deep:
the depths of my deepest misery
calls unto the depths of your highest
mercy. Looking for the ground on
which to stand, a place on which to
grasp, I find nothing but you. . .


Where then? In love. There is His
resting place. And He whom you look
for, since He is in your love, is in
your self. And if He is not in
your love, is not in you.

He whom you look for you would
not seek, if you did not love Him.
So, you have the one you look for,
and He is in your self.

# BLOND FRANZ, THE FAMOUS NIGHT SILO SITTER

Blond Franz the famous night silo sitter
high on the moonbeams that flood his soul
*"Come down,"* they shout from the dark below. . .
*"No, man, I like it like it is."*

It is like when two friends sit
and watch a fox trot across the meadow,
count the cloud fleece sheep skin the pines
or twiddle their minds to make believe
gold crowns rested on the trees by the morning sun.

*"Come down,"* they shout.
*"No, man, I like it like it is."*

Blond Franz Michelangelo's David in disguise
high on the grace that floods his soul
always out of his head for other people,
reaches his hand to those not knowing how it is.

It is like when two hearts meet
looking in an outward direction,
share their blood for a hurting brother,
spill over in joy for a new-made mother,
pound to the beat of a Love so great
as to take away the need of telling each other.

*"Come down,"* they shout.
*"No, man, I like it like it is."*

# CANDLEMAS

beads of my life force
drip from the candle
fusing past and now
candlemas burning flesh
purity of desire
montage of light and
dark forms
arms and legs and memories
bodies agonies

could it be my tears
were yours
from closeness?

# I ASK NO EXPLANATIONS

Beating against the granite rock of life
with rage and soft words
I stand atop it
and feel the waves of fear crash
at my feet against my knees and through me

Sirens crash against my ears
alien night sounds
tear against the gratings of my tears

I ask no explanations
but tell me why you stay silent
while I beat in hurt for you
tell me why I cannot say
no to them and yes to you
or bridge this gulf of wailing

I ask no explanations
but tell me why I hate them
who lean against my chest
and smash their hands from me
as they reach to touch

I ask no explanations
but why this growing shadow between our meeting
and these defeating flames that burn
the waters of my mind
yearning for those I cannot have
and something I don't wish

I ask no explanations
but why stand I steady against this crushing chaos
and this rock a spring-time mound
of clay and grass and hope
and jonquils swaying in the blue breeze
of my existence not them nor there but now

I ask no explanations
but why this surge of joy amidst such sadness
and a forest of feeling flung open to the
clouds and birds and light
why this turning of my heart to further hurt
for you


# SOLEMN PROFESSION: FOR A BROTHER MONK

PSALM 139

How ever would you have known, my son
from before you were born I loved you
and fashioned you in your Mother's womb
with a face of light and eyes to touch.

Why never did you guess you danced
in my hand while you thought yourself nowhere
and roamed discontented seeker of your mind
and a human heart big enough to fill you.

How ever could you have judged yourself
my own heart's love instead, wept for
in your pain and kept from this life's happiness
for your Eternal Beatitude.

My Blessed, precious, Little Son, Come.


# MIRIAM ALONG THE LAKESIDE

Miriam along the
lakeside and a
tall fisher-of-men
giant Jesus smiling Uncle
tossing bread to
the guppies of Gennesaret
and smiles to
the glistening liquid
eyes of the water child
who follows behind
in equal step
tossing her hands
in imitation
of his gestures
Miriam along the
lakeside
little wonder
you enchant
your giant Jesus smiling Uncle


# FLESH OF MY SOUL

You alone know me and
probe me and scrutinize me
turn whatever it is
inside me that will reveal
my mystery to myself
ever turn me back to you

## "LAND OF ENCHANTMENT"

New Mexico, Land of Enchantment
where rioting prisoners use
shovels to kill
*'sex or blood on the*
*knife'* is your choice
and melt prisoners' genitals
with blow torches
flowering yucca
and dope streams
*'all they'd find left behind*
*would be your glasses'*

shipwreck rock and
bloodied toilets
luminaries at night
lightning over *Sandia*
thunder and *Sangre de Cristo*
sloping into nightmares of heat
bejewelled cities from above
and apocalyptic explosions at
Los Alamos

D. H. Lawrence and super-sexed
teenagers at the Albuquerque bus station
church steeple like tin witch's cap
and swimming pools full of dark skin 'lovelies'
Guadalupe's Virgin in a thousand apparitions
plastic and *bultos*, painted and soft-toned
*'Speak lightly as you read'* and *'quit*
*while we're ahead'* like lines from Ferlinghetti
Trini Lopez teenage boys with bongos and
guitars and dope in their brains

# YOU CANNOT COME

*"We have become partners in Christ if only we maintain to the end that confidence with which we began."*

HEBREWS 3:14

*

You cannot come because then you would go
and leave me to an empty tomorrow
you no longer need me
there is nothing for you here
but happy memories for friendship's sake

You have your adulation and
purpose for living for others
and your situations and positions
to protect you
while I choose to seek to embrace
a life apart, alone, a wilderness
existence

to love alone as solitary lover what
always must seem an abstraction
to seek to embrace a life always to be
a noble failure

and naked memories of life
like a ranch somewhere in Wyoming
a false return to true exchanges
in the past where life
never really hurt
or better perhaps a true return to
false exchanges

We all need our own truth
you no longer need me
I need to sit alone awhile
to maybe tease peace into
staying with me

We need to bring Jesus to others
He who is our life's love
while we each seek to live for Him
you His song in your mouth
your skin His to touch by them
while I am somehow His silence
and His fast from human comfort

You bring Him you be Him in
word and gesture
I will be His silence
You be His touch.  I will be His solitude.
You be His presence.  I will be His
desert separation.
You be His song.  I will be His
wilderness stillness.

You no longer need me
and I need to sit alone awhile
to maybe try to tease peace
into staying with me awhile

In the end, I guess, we are always alone
in another way, as you say, we are
never alone
with others, as you say, we are always
alone
with Him we are never alone

Let us always strive to love Him first
let us always be Him for others
partnership and perseverance—not
lovers, brothers or sisters in the human
sense

His song be in your mouth.  Your skin
His to touch by them.
Bring Him in Word and presence and
deepening love, in gesture of caring.

To truly believe in grace as personal
change, as forgiveness of the past
and possibility for the future
if only to the end we persevere
in vows of poverty of identity, my
hand His to mend from a distance

to experience Life's nakedness with
another close to a cabin in what must
be a Wyoming of the memory, my
pristine consciousness and lamented
*naïveté*

Your smile mocks away my sorrow
You, always sure, with your gentle smile
Others have loved me
You alone have held me

The *via negativa* is not fun
but it is the way to freedom
monastic joy is so much like zero
hushed joys and silent unexpected
graves
infinite completely quiet, neutral emotions
so much like bliss consciousness, so
much like depression

Ah, flesh of my soul, you alone know
me and probe me and scrutinize me
with your steadfast eyes
turn whatever it is inside me
that will reveal my mystery to myself
ever turn me back to you and from
you to Him

I need to go inside myself
to find I don't exist
in the many ways imagined

in my ignorance
nor do you
as imagined in my need
a pattern of dependencies

It's not *"get psyched," "get stoned," "get
laid." "Go it alone"* is the best way to say it
a solo flight to independence
from the opinions of others
from ourselves
free-functioning active agent—all alone
little *satoris* after long chewings
on this iron *koan* called "LIFE"
*"I can go deeper than many here,"*
said the disciple.
*"Still deluded!"* said the Master.
*"You must free yourself from the obligation
of sanity."*
"You can live freely with the 'crazies'
who surround you here."

For months to chew on iron
and then in minutes
to pass from page to page through books
from door to door to door in
passageways
from insight to insight to insight

waves of oceans in the grass
measured against the grains
of my past deserts
alone I walk a path
once travelled with other companions
and count the cost of persons
in my life

You cannot come, but please pray for
me, happy friend, for my vocation
and that I better know myself
Someway we will be together again

Now I am still too weak and
undetermined within myself, and I
don't want to deflect you from your
path

I feel the need to protect you and
the need for more distance from
experiences of growth in the past

I fumble along trying my best at
each stage and looking back realize
I could have done so much better,
but don't give up, don't stop
I hope you understand and know
of my gratitude.
You cannot come because then you
would go and leave me
to an empty tomorrow

I at least want to exercise some free
decisions for both our goods
as I inch along.
I need to go inside myself
to know the truth of poverty of
work in routine, dull, monotonous
rhythms of ordinariness day to day,
at the same hours, from intellect
to feelings at least, from abstractions
to the first fruits of new experience
no escape! feeling the feelings without
the pretenses
no place to go. No place to run
Saying: *"I should be somewhere else by
now: priest, professed, father, employed. . .!"*

No other accomplishment either.
Just being here, nowhere

If only to the end we persevere
in knowing our own, truth
who is Him.

# EVOCATION #1

Catching the dawn from an all-night cafe in a one-taxi town
stirring the sugar in, *"Oh, mama, my mind turns to you."*

*"Ain't it funny, Honey, how we throw*
*away our words like trash*
*instead of thrashing away the night*
*the way we used to do."*

This coffee's getting cold. I sit silent like the poet who stared at
his cup, then said: *"Would it help if I speak Spanish?"* So, I'll
say:

*"¡Señorita, ayúdame, por favor!*
*tu eres para mi una hermanita muy querida*
*pero tenemos un problema*
*no puedo comprender todo lo que tu haces..."*

*"Yes, please, and some more sugar too."*

The spoon-swayed liquid circles my mind to the time I met you.

*"Oh, how you appeared the perfect one*
*white to your ankles in lace and a straw hat*
*God, that brown hair (and the wheat fields) on the Greyhound bus*
*somewhere south of San Francisco towards L.A.*
*how, as we stepped out, you tapped*
*me on the shoulder."* *"Hello, silent one!"*
*"I swore then I'd never lose you*
*intoxicated by your gentleness*

*trying to hide my dirty shoes*
*exposed by your scented smile."*

*"Yes, I will have some more. Thank you."*

Miles away in an all-night cafe. Days away from you
*"Damn, where are you, Honey?"*

So to my cup I say: *"Would it help it I spoke in Latin?"*

*"Tu scis quia amo te!"*

*"But hell, that's a line after another man's betrayal*
*and you've heard it so many times before."*

*"Waitress, yes, I think I need another.*
*Just make it black this time."* I guess
I already know her answer
and I just have to take it bitter,
at least for a while.


## PURUSA

*Purusa,* once I saw you pat your Daddy
on the rear and tears flooded my flushed
face in witnessing it—the Child caressing
the Father, the Son reassuring Dad in a time
of parting—.

Stand you alone so sensitive one once having
found out the silken care of womanly love
and the adulation of friendships false and
so surprisingly sometimes true, true aspects of
the Truth you so passionately seek—.

Build your room deep and build it strong
you are young and capable of it while it
is time—it is your very soul—yet
a door out and in and windows for
light and the freshness of unburdening
disturbances—.

In some way make your room
the Vastness of God.

# A MINISTER'S WOES

from the bench
traffic jam sunset
talks of Resurrection
seeing Buddha in
a blade of grass

how fond you were
in the snowfall
of our parting

stolen touches in
the toilets
blood
splattered
across the room

your wife would only
let you come
with simple contractions
of your muscles

in your rage


# A SON'S PERSPECTIVE

Pine trees (fir trees) hanging upside down
in the breezeway
home-made
foil shrine for the Virgin
wooden trellises
Cameron Highlanders and Coldstream Guards
my first beer—"root beer"
The Virgin's mantle around you

## CHRISTOPHER

I wrote a poem for you when you were born
it is gone now and you are bigger
You looked like Jesus in your crib
except for your striped baseball
two piece play suit & baseball insignia
I made a clown doll for you because you
were my joy in difficult times
I played guitar songs with my friends
to announce your first birthday party
I give you that guitar now because
maybe someday it will mean something
to you just to get a gift from love for you


## THOUSAND COLORED BIRD: A TRANSLATION FROM THE SPANISH VERSION OF A POEM BY GARBAL

*"Yo he sido un ave aprisionada entre rejas de viento que tenían la tangibilidad
del acero, según lo creía mi ignorancia. ¡Vuela, pájaro demil colores, vuela, ave
maravillosa, hacia tu Patria celeste! ¡Abre bien los ojos, no te detengas frente
a los barrotes de tu celda que ellos tan sólo existen en tu miedo mental!"*

I have been a bird imprisoned
behind confines of air
which in my ignorance
seemed so much like iron.

Flee! Thousand-colored bird.
Flee! Marvelous bird
to your homeland above.

Open full your eyes.
Be not held bound
by prison bars
made real only
by your fear-filled mind.

## WAR GAMES

Snap fast the elastic artillery
topple the tin-cast grenadier
in silver *cuirasse* and bearskin
wound from shoulder to foot
in cords and leather straps and sashings
sited up above a cupboard
duck quick the return
of imaginary fire
hold-fast your station
hold-high your troop's colours
and ignore the tolling
of the bed-time clock


## SUFFICIENT *ZEN*

The crescent moon
a jet
an evening swallow
late Spring
cloister view. . .


## GRADUALLY TURN OUT THE LIGHTS OF IMAGINATION

Double image in the East window
glass as the moon is lifted from
the vest-pocket of the night
gold grandfather's watch on a chain
of stars and red set venus bob

Lights across the ridge of my
memory cars your jeweled bracelet
sways montage of your eyes
beads of my life force
drip from the candle fusing

past and now candlemas
burning flesh purity of desire
dark forms arms legs bodies
agonies

Could it be my tears are your
from closeness?

Planets move like planes
in the night flame fire to
my room lantern frames of envy
bright lights and vibrations
constellation of feelings
conflagration in the night
like sunrises hiding in the
roots of moonlight.

Silence drapes like your velvet
midnight great opera cape trimmed
in ermine the white satin lining
of your sensitivities

Could it be your tears are mine
from distance?


# EXAMINING OTHER PEOPLE'S REALITIES

The Philadelphia hip-street-talker
with one balloon in the air
another under the floorboards
never had time for a sheepskin
says it's a miracle he's still within
space and time without dependents
since *'time is so spacy!'*
blew out his wheels in Poughkeepsie
wanted still in Jersey for a minor
misdemeanor being mildly offensive
in their clear air
never travelled the South alone
for fear of a rap on 'vagrancy'

143

airport hero of the Mardi Gras
when asked:
*"What right do you have to be so thin?"*
says
*"Thin is in at the beach this year. I'm
just being fashionable."*
Helped deliver a baby to mother cow by
moonlight
long-hair gold pony-tailed dream arguing with
*gurus*
photo at fire engine in phosphorescent yellow
halloween pumpkin in the cloister


# THE SMILE AND THE SCIMITAR

1. Moon:
smile of the
Cheshire Cat.

2. Moon:
Our Lady's
scimitar
and
jewelled
scabbard.


# MR. CLEAN DEAN

Mr. Clean Dean with his clothes
all in plastic bags, with zippers!

I'm not the type to
sit around
trading household hints
on how to wipe
your formica tops
in the kitchen

## CHANGE

a movement in the
constellations stars from
dog to cow
you know how much I
like change
especially at cash registers


## SAID THE CHAIR

*"I am considerably (very) reserved,"*
said the chair, lacking a
*"do not sit on me"* sign.
*(¡No me disturbe, por favor!)*


## YOU ALMOST CAN'T FEEL IT

It's so hot it burns your skin.
It's so hot you almost can't feel it.
The appearance of a muppet with the heart of God.
Yoga postures must not be seen through
a mirror but from within.


## SAID THE BIG FLOWER

*"Do nothing until you hear from me,"* said the Big Flower
to his disciple, Superspats, whose poetry the
Benedictine nun used to start a marshmallow roast.

## RIDDLES

*"I just laid a sidewalk,"* he said innocently enough.
*"You really are into some weird experiences, aren't you?"*
*"I just laid a sidewalk,"* said Jack Hammer.
*"You sure are into some weird experiences,"* said Simon Eyes.


## MERIDIAN: WHEN THE SUN IS UP

How 'bout it, Baby, just
now and then
just you and me now and then
with nobody else knowing
now and then
no strings attached
no questions asked
no responsibilities
no "hellos" in recognized situations
no cards no gifts
no calls in between
just a quiet time
now and then for comfort
nobody would get hurt
just a day away
now and then when we're able
no questions asked
no damage done
no wounded feelings
just to get together
now and then
How 'bout it, Baby,
just now and then?

It's crazy!

# EVOCATION #2

In your dreams
you see her like
a sun-bleached stream
and feel your life
pulled from you by her.

You hear her
like a prairie woman say:
*"How I dreamed of you*
*warm, slow like the storm that rose*
*hesitant before the thunderclap*
*spilled and faded in the distance."*

# DEAR DIANA

Dear Diana with your
loom-like upright harp
and the sun beaming through
your golden hair

I rock in your chair
and reel and read
your verse
and marvel at it all

# I'M PULLIN' AWAY FROM THE 60'S

I'm pullin' away from the 60's
like a wearied ten-year bridegroom
after the rolls have
been hard-won and the
games gone down bad

How much I've been filled by
unflattering reminders

of the best and worst times
I've had and so much
unwanted change
left over

For me you are as much as
I know
forget you knew me
it'll make it easier
for both of us that way

Youth-love, love of my youth
paid full in hard rolls of
flash and fiction

I've got the feelin' you think
I'm not your kind of guy
your kindness must be kept
for someone else instead

It hurts to be mistrusted
It hurts after how much we tried
It hurts so much I'm busted up inside


## CURIOUS MENTORS

1. There is NOWHERE to go to find
   what you are looking for.

2. The grasshopper and the lady spider
   one to prey on the other.  Awareness leads
   to connection.

3. Do not try to correlate.  Just be at
   the stage of absorption.

4. Face the future without you.

5. Who has compassion on the ill physician?

6. You are to wear nothing that is of leather  
   nothing that is shiny, nothing unbefitting a monk.

7. Do you take pride in your self-knowledge?

8. A dose of your own sophism never hurts.

9. Don't rush back to Denmark. Between Scandinavia  
   and Canadian bus trips you'll almost lose your mind.

10. The heir does not earn.

11. *"You were always restless. I never."*  
    *"For what?"* you say. *"For whom?"* I ask.

12. Anxiety shuts everything down: energies  
    to look ahead, remembrance (past and future).  
    Resemblance. Anxiety is unbelief.

13. Politics is deeper than the common man.

14. At least don't be a synchophant.

15. Is this just another one of your spontaneous  
    circuses?

16. You can't remember when you didn't know him.

17. You locked me in your antique treasure chest  
    to suffocate of dust and gloom.

18. Build a tabernacle around an experience.

19. Assume that you know less about another than  
    you think. Personhood is never exhausted.

20. Assume others know more about you than you  
    have realized. We constantly reveal ourselves and  
    are revealed by others.

21. Yet realize that others know less about you than  
    they might imagine.

# LIFE WITH THE CRAZIES

1. Good ribbons, manners in dark skins, glued ribbons,
   to the glab, blab past.

2. Zucchini quick, my little *cucaracha* from Madagascar.

3. Feeble fables flottin' swies *Gemitzka* (meek and mild)
   make the better bad. That's good!

4. Merlin *le Gout,* the condensed tomato, my mind's
   a zoo, too.

5. Cross country drive to an international tell-all about
   the non-influence of Kafka on the Check Blue Army.

6. Did you note that? Righting broken lines.

7. Galinda and Malisaphant pals in *QUONDAM* glasses.

8. *"I am considerably yours,"* said I. *"I am reserved,"*
   said the chair.

9. *"If you don't think much of the place, you never think
   of it,"* said the curio cabinet.

10. Blackout: squash milk, cooking in the dark.

11. What's in a truck ride, anyway?

12. Just one of your myriad satellites. . .

13. Are you an irredeemable dunce?

14. Are you a porphyry vessel of perfection?

15. Accentuate your ugliness!

16. I was remembering the year you had all the mirrors
    hanging from the arch: Glory! Glory!

17. My brain fogs up every time I cross the Chattahoochee.

18. Wish I weren't dead in my head. Don't want gloom to spread. Hope to think of you instead.

19. Food chain: the union of the can with the mouse. *"I love mice!"*

20. Have you read the *YUPRUVDYURPASSUNTSTUMI SUTRA?*

21. If you *vis* to *transire conmigo esta tarde* just drop me a *waka* or two.

22. He puts his glasses on to look at his rings and other things. He is the banana-bearer for the Arch-Prince Prelate.

23. A stint with a squirrel.

24. You, a clown on the back of a seahorse.

25. *Metanoia:* Mertonitis. Pseudo-xenophobia.

26. *C'est la vie! Viva Gesu!* New beer.

# HALF-WAY THERE IS NOT THERE

1. I evolved from a monkey to a monk and lost my tale.

2. The mechanical lion. Sconce. Power and light: artificial energy.

3. Tufts of *moiré* and a collar pin. Great Jehoshophat!

4. Transcendental mantra chanters.

5. My choir stall is my *Zen* cushion. Stability: marginal man, physical dependence on environment, stability to Truth, concerned with Absolutes, transported culture. Personal journey.

6. Evenings of memories and images.

7. Blue mood. November trees.

8. The light, the moth, the frog, the snake, the man afraid.

9. The white-tailed heron. The fuschia-mouthed lizard.

10. From the moment of the beginning.


## POSITIVE HALLUCINATIONS

1. Nothing in there you can't see.

2. Bubber Gum Rap.

3. My knees and my nephew.

4. See that you see yourself often. *Intermezzo.*

5. Implied rejection from a high-tech duck.

6. Surely there should be some poems from Chicago.

# ST. JOHN'S STEEPLE OR WHILE
# THE THEOLOGIANS STUDY

Steepled streets in the night-time rain
clang out glass and car horns
to dissonant factory whistles

like a long-legged Egyptian foreign to
myself I wander unknown places
passing perverts and dungeons of
pleasure on my way to downtown churches
my thoughts like Hispanics fighting
in the east New York streets
of my memory and darkened tomorrow

like the sea rolling in his wedding bed
I marry nightmare feelings with pious
devotion and like a young monk baking
Holy Bread I pretend not to hear
the breaking of the waves within me

young groom named the sea
rolled in his marriage bed
and broke in a wave of pleasure
slammed the rocks with a wave of bliss
spilled on her seashore

like candles of wishful thinking I project
sin on city lights and with the help
of the Roman Catholic chronicle my birth
in bursts of purple lips and fingers
flares of confusion and moral uncertainties
striped like deacons' stoles
across my sensibilities

St. John's steeple clinging, clanging glass
neon rows along the roads and
sidewalks to the street-hiss mists and
wheels turning

East Georgia Street whores look more
like sisters and bless old women as
they wend their rounds past *La Scala*
Restaurant and pawn shops near
Union Station where timid boys hand
out their beauty and bewildered priests
head for the Chancery

Steepled streets in the night-time rain
clang out glass and car horns to
dissonant factory whistles

St. John's steeple clinging, clanging glass
neon rows along the roads and sidewalks
to the street-hiss mist and wheels turning

tight-wound like a snare drum tapping
the rain my fingers clench and form a
spider around the frail, white, wren's egg
undeserved Eucharist as ostrich plumes
promenade along the trestles near
Convention Center and railways keep silent
vigil to the immensity of my moaning

from rote I recite *sutras* and search
their parallels for revelation of my
meaning

and St. John's steeple punctures the
night-time sky
clinging, clanging, dangling from the
night-time sky
ringing, ranging, wringing out glass
neon lights as the street-hiss mists
rise

Steepled streets in the night-time rain
clang out glass and car horns
to dissonant factory whistles

I pass places where a Rimbaud might
meet his sad fame and *verbatim*
situations, except for the mastery of
his words

Indiana Theatre in the rain and neon
stream busses pass like analysts and
play into their own weakness: *"We
cannot expect you to do what we ask
when those around you want no part
of such honesty."* And my own
hardness always an act at a time
when too timid just to say *'virginity'*

*Religionwissenshaft* notebooks and a
school-boys's dream trying to be tough
Edwardian double-breasted long coat,
white leather vest, cravat and black
silk top-hat cherry-red face and
guitar axe

out of this vale of costumes I live
a circus (of *Salve Reginas*) in my head
and drop acid comments on my own
protectors claiming even I could come
from somewhere

*"Why don't you preach?"* the undergraduates
ask. *"Because I practice!"* I retort and
feel the shame of my lie a hostile
youth resentful of life and Divinity's
intrusion

St. John's steeple, clinging, clanging glass
neon rows along the roads and sidewalks
to the street-hiss mists and wheels turning

Through BLOCK'S fabric bins of black crepe
and fuschia taffeta, green knits and
checkered wool, houndstooth and herring-bone
and antique satins, from foil-wrapped
perfumes to the mezzanine for morocco-bound

155

books of the humor and wisdom of
Lucifer's unwitting children driven by
their unnamed emotions made wild by
their untamed imaginations

Monuments circle to the long-lost dead and
steeple streets in the night-time rain
clang out neon glass and car horns
to dissonant factory whistles

the creepy intelligence behind the angry,
insulted eyes of the storefront painted
mannequins who suddenly move and my
life like a chain of *ibidems* to other
persons' wishes hostile and resentful
of their drain and in Troys without
a Helen hoarse from screaming to the
rhythm of the streetcars played on
wooden-veneer tables with 12 string
flat-picks through picture glass to
the steepled streets in the night-time rain

Glad for Rensselaer sunsets in my mind
and marching bands in bushbies,
nights when piano player wooed his lady
once again to melodies in my own
listening while his chemistry painted
the patterns on his corduroys
the building with calliope and all
one day burned to the ground except
for the music scored in three memories
and a scene in a film about a
white ace hero athlete dying in the arms
of his black-spade friend

out of this vale of costumes I live a
circus (of *Salve Reginas)* in my head
and drop acid on my own sensibilities
to protect my detractors

And St. John's steeple, clinging clanging
glass neon rows along the roads and
sidewalks to street-hiss mists and
wheels turning

enter athletes and the plaid-draped boys
East Washington Street like London fog
as the lights turn from red to green
I glance back and feel again the tugging
in my chest as I reach the rain-drenched
curb toward East Virginia Avenue

tousled hair in the rain
and Strauss pale-blue pin-striped suits
and lions flaming from cars like from
a poet's pen with laughing giraffe
phrases on sidewalk canvasses and
parchments I turn to see my footprints
disappear

And St. John's Church and steepled streets
in the night-time rain clang out glass
and car horns to the dissonant factory
whistles and railway vigils and buses
and mannequins all remind me:

*"You cannot demand affection,"*
as I reply
*"Even I could come from somewhere!"*

St. John's steeple and a vocabulary of
mindfulness and *mahabodhisattvas*
grapes and wheat carved in the canopied
oak pulpit Eucharist-Word, Presence-Proclamation
symbolized Nativity near the
Baptistery and marble railings and
stars on blue a parody of processions
through my mind: *cloisonné* cups and
crock-ware vessels Abbots in *cacullas*
and cords of gold entwined with black
prelates in magenta *mantelletas* and satin-
cuffed *rochets* made of Swedish lace

157

*'ECCE SACERDOS'* trumpets to a mitre of damask
and *bugia* bearers, *ceroferarii, calceaferarii*
*gremiale* carriers with lemon and bread squares

the anonymity of defection and disaffection
for once to be ministered to

*'siren night, howling night, all are overcome*
*with fright'*

processions through my head after the
ceremony the liturgy of life continues

*dires irae, hanc igitur, te decet laus*
*missa coram populo/missa pro me*
*liber usualis* and *totum* breviaries

And St. John's steeple clings to the night-
time sky cleaves to rainbows of neon
rows flashing. '*WHY*?'
Keats in the rain: *"Whose name was*
*writ in water"* and the *TAO*: *"He who*
*shows himself is not conspicuous."*

Indiana Church Supply, parking lots empty
like few-figured ledgers of friendship,
companionship, a frenzy of crap and
shattered Ripple bottles strew the alleyways
of responsibility with crud and cockroaches
paper bags and needles past *terra cotta*
*poverello* and silk-rimmed banners to the
Virgin (Krieg's). St. Elmo's Steak House and
a hotel for maimed veterans, white niggers
in their own self-esteem spitting and other
outcasts of society welcome me to their
all-too-familiar haunts.

Great Fidelity and Christ Church Cathedral
with its heraldic shield, haberdashers and
hashish vendors and pimps pushing

their half-hour wares by the
WOOLWORTH'S phone booth PENNY'S WASSON'S
CIRCLE THEATRE—exclusive club

equestrian signals pace the fragmented flow
of traffic and chemicals *foso*-moats
catch the drift of pedestrians *"making
the better bad"* by alchemies of nature
and good temperaments: *mis riñones vibran*
and the bells serve as *cicerone* guide
through the soaking night

WARREN HOTEL first place the Sojourners
played and sitting nearby at night time
men we were in the street

BARTON HOTEL memories of missionary China
Bishop, O.F.M., in gray cassock and grosgrain
sash with tassel met at Little Sisters of
the Poor during Holy Week then here for
100th Anniversary celebration of St. John's
Church—how he described to me the
sufferings in China—memories evoked by
the *T'ang* and *Sung* landscape scrolls
and Chinese block-prints on the *foyer*
walls

UNION STATION this massive tomb shudders
under the wheels of the iron coffins,
place of New Year's Eve galas: Like
mauve plumes, dusk dangling, crepe-myrtle
musketeers, martial youths in button-
down colored slacks like medieval
codpieces modern Montagues thumbing
their noses at other rogues and chasing
chic Capulets in Queen Ann's lace
chaplets, nosing their thumbs into the
prettiest ones, Princes and foxes, Caesar's
and Borgias, maps and knights in
*morions* on each fly-leaf of their copy

159

book bindings, *tyros* of youth and
Tyrone Power fit for 'MILLION DOLLAR MOVIES'
boys with green hair and Green Dolphin
Street, Alan Ladds and lucky lasses
in dangling tresses of auburn, scenes

that would make Oscar Wilde weep for
their beauty, and tragedy, and his own
twisted, miserable self-hate

In Union Station I consort with a dark
Spanish Lady and her escort half her
size:

*"Nada te turbe, nada te espante, todo se pasa,*
*Dios no se muda.  La paciencia todo lo alcanza;*
*quien a Dios tiene nada le falta:  Sólo Dios basta."*

*"He who has need for no one has many friends."*

*NADA TE TURBE #9* and her friend, *Juanito,*
*'El Senequito'* who tells me:

*"Por eso es gran negocio para el alma ejercitar en esta*
*vida los actos de amor, porque consumándose en breve,*
*no se detenga mucho acá o allá sin ver a Dios."*

*"Do not be detained, do not linger here*
*and there"* and how easy to read
while so many things bait the appetite
of pride and inferiority during this
*UNA NOCHE OSCURA/CALUROSA* of life.

St. John's Rectory: *Ming* vases on the mantle
and iron grilles. *"You are not crazy,*
*but seek the historical study, not the*
*practice, of Zen if you wish to be a*
*member of the Archabbey Community.*
*I have no clairvoyance or 'gift' of*
*discernment in your vocation."*

160

Things remain as they are.  They change
and stay the same.  When the bell rings,
it rings.  Things are just as they are,
and needs remain the same, as the
bells ring.  Suffering from a lack of
too much love, a thirst for a lack
of too much water

To gradually turn out the lights of
imagination.  To surrender to the depths
of your deep dark feelings that open
like the close of a blue-gray day
to a bombast of silence and darkness
when looking for approval

I'm no Rimbaud.  I don't have the balls to
scrawl *"Shit on God!"* though I scream
it through my soul.  I am at base a
monist.  I believe, in the end, after all
our misery and our joys everything will
be even and all will be won by all.

Surprised by EVIL?  *"Never!"*
By GOODNESS?  *"Yes!"*
By HATE?  *"Never!"*
By TRUE LOVE?  *"Yes, what is that?"*

And steepled streets in the night-time
rain clang out glass and car horns
to dissonant factory whistles
and St. John's Church against the night-
time sky clings, clangs out against the
glass neon mist and car-wheel hiss
rising

*"I'm the only canonical cleric in the
group but everyone else but me is
wearing a Roman collar,"* I remember
saying, and added: *"I hear that Japanese
women are wonderful lovers."* *"How
would I know?"* said he and went on

to describe *Ikebana* and the proper
pronunciation of *Tokyo*: *"Not three
syllables but two, please."*

I parodied myself with paradoxes, ironies,
stationery from Abbey Press with
"WHAT'S THE GOOD WORD?" [printed
red on blue] to announce my delay
of entrance into the Novitiate, or
Oriental landscape prints sent to the
Novice Master: *"Hope all is well with
the novices. . .Thank you for all you
have done for me!"*

Inferiority debates with myself: *"Why
ask me to play guitar for you
when he is available? Why take
silver when you can have gold!"* I
told the Dean of Men—and we all broke
into *"THE KING OF GLORY,"* or in response
to compliments after playing a
meditation song for the Archbishop:
*"My guitar was not properly tuned!"*

Ah yes, I want to be like all the other
guys but my g.d. personality won't
let me. All the ironies of life.
*"A monk is not ordained before his time."*
My love acts are with God in mystical
Union: *"I'm sure He enjoys it!"* came
your response.
Oh God, I've looked for you in so many
people and so many places, from the
William Penn Hotel to the *mesas* of the
Ojai Valley frenzied *'push the panic
button'* cleric and self-hate trips for
the seminarian on vacation, digital
clocks and auto-stimulation, Chinese
calligraphy and long-distance calls
home

St. John's steeple clinging, clanging glass neon
rows along the roads and sidewalks to
the street-hiss mist and wheels turning
Go out now all athletes and blond-haired
friends, all thoughts of tousled-haired
youth and ball-players, all tuggers at my chest
and plaid-clad friends, pseudo-friends?
*"Are you really interested in me for me?"*
*"I don't hate you,"* you say, *"but it is
a problem!"* Go out now all rain-
drenched curbs, London Fog coats and
colored lights. *"Do you consider me a
leech?"* Go out now long-legged Egyptian
and mannequins, all fighting Hispanics
of my mind, roll yourself to sleep sea,
sweet lover of the night young groom
of regained innocence, go out now all
street whores and pimps and lost school
boys, fabric vendors and scholars, prelates
pass peacefully into the night of memory
all *mahabodhisattvas,* all outcasts, pretty
boys and mateless Capulets, go now my
Carmelite companions, *Zen* nuts and
literary figures, all voices of consolation
and lights of imagination

fade now St. John's steeple into the
night-time sky, your silver, silent
sentinel, redemptive tragedy is no longer
needed. The *I* of *me* teeters along the
edge of faith, the tear-stained taffeta
sheet of memory, the giddiness of mind
and shredding of heart. The *ME* of *me*
now believes and knows and loves.

## NOT ANYMORE

*"I may not come."*
*"That would be a first."*
*"Not anymore!"* *"Can't you just*
*write a normal letter like*
*everyone else does. Not every*
*letter has to be for publication."*

## THEY

They slept together for the first time
in Virginia.
They never touched and hardly spoke in D.C.
In New York City they were interested
in others and
slept apart.
In Niagara they slept in someone else's
room.
In Detroit they watched with awe
as they stirred
silent in the morning.

164

# MY *CONFIDANTÉ*

I broke a lilac branch after school and took you to the circus.
We were too squeamish to watch the boa constrictor and settled for
mechanical witches and some candy for the walk home.

You gave me popcorn evenings and street lights to mark the
coming of the night. *"You better get home." "It's time to leave!"*
I gave you word games and played *'house'* as your loving *'hubby.'*

Our play was innocent enough, little war games.
I wore a home-made scarlet coat. You sewed the brass buttons and
black felt facing. I triumphed in imaginary skirmishes.
You healed my little school-boy wounds.

You gave me a scimitar in a sheath of red velvet, a brass *aftabah*
with finely carved-out rosebuds, tinted green and pink, and an
auto-harp and boots of suede, florentine memories bound in tooled
leather.

I gave you attention and hand-made tapestries for your room,
pumpkin-dream fairy tales and my latest discoveries in Sanskrit and a
Welsh balladeer, lectures on the perennial philosophy.

You gave me Tolkien's mystic music and language scripts, Sacred
Scriptures on onion skin and a deep tolerance of my stretching,
searching mind, and imaginary nights.

I gave you closed-eyed mornings a next day's work, tickets to
concerts tours through our family history and the city's
bookstores and a life-time of heart-wrenching memories.

You gave me a Japanese tea set with delicate palm-size rice
leaf-patterned bowls and wicker handles, kumquats served on
a Steuben glass dish, some books on Spanish mystics of the
Sacred Heart, modern liturgical music and a kaleidoscope
carpet from which to sing.

I gave you a Chinese brush-pen box, a treasure from my
Grandmother, black-lacquered with frail faded courtesans outlined in
gold. I was your company and your confidante.

You gave me feminine sympathy, a soothing of my hurts, a place of heart to rest. I wrote letters to you from a farm-framed valley creek and thanked you with poems in winter time.

In early days you were idealized. I wrote embarrassing poems and the promise of my modesty. I think you were disappointed. Later I lusted for you, with blue jeans and baby nestled on your hip, and knew for the first time the true meaning of Jesus' words about what goes on in a man's heart and mind, though not in his actions.

You gave me recordings of the electric Rimbaud, a sense of my own growth and desire for God. I gave you Carmelite treatises on prayer in black paper-bindings, a book of someone else's meditations by the sea, and your own rediscovery of who you really are.

# THE ROYAL WEDDING OF THE PRINCE OF WALES

today the prince of wales
will wed
and seek a night of solace in his bed
from all the cares and woes
of State
with lovely Diana his
royal mate


# THE CARS COME DOWN LIKE VIRGINS:
# TRAPPIST ABBEY, MORNING

MATTHEW 25:1-13

The cars come down like virgins
in the early morning twilight
and with their lamps
light the hearts of lonesome monks
foolish and sleepy-eyed
wending their way
to meet their Christ
in Eucharist
and the new day.


\*


Your love and goodness is
always with us here
like precious oil on our
way to Him.

# THE MISSISSIPPI DRIFTS: A REMINISCENCE

The Mississippi drifts
we sit
in the Illinois
rain


# ROCKS & BRICKS

You brought back
a rock
from the *Schnitzelbanch*.
I went
to throw it
away
and made you
cry.
Your sister
hit you
in the mouth
with a brick.

# DARK VIRGIN OF *AVELINO*

O Virgin of Avelino *aracoeli*
icon of our family,
Byzantine almond eyes and
Hebrew Jewish nose,
window to our souls,
diadem of gold and rubies,
earth-shattering,
sheltering Madonna, keeping
all these things
in your heart.
In all our needs,
we beseech thee,
never let us go.

Be with me always
I beg you.  My own self-love
and inward concern confuses
the love I wish to give you.
Allow me to express
my great joy of heart in knowing
of your loving care for me
and all our family.
You always hear the good
take the good,
discard all that is weak
and selfish in my loving.

The sadness of this life's
separation it makes me
offer myself through you again
to my Lord your Son.
In this life I seek to live,
there is always a gulf of
separation.  The monk must live
alone from all others, lovers,
brothers, family, and
left-behind friends.

*

O Virgin of Avelino, *arapacis*
icon of our family.
I feel this so deeply because
of my need for human comfort.
Can you understand me, Lady?
May my need for you increase
as my need for others lessens.
Teach me renunciation and peace
in your son, Jesus, as I promise
to give myself to Him and live
for you and all others in Him.

How can I think of life without You?
Separation deepens my regard for you,
whom I so much take for granted as I
so quickly put my needs before all
others' needs each day here.
In prayer and in silent communion,
be for all of us a miracle of quiet
and guidance and peacefulness, in this
monastery and wherever we might be.

O Virgin of Avelino, *aracrucis*,
icon of our family.
I want to be a saint. Such an
astounding desire!
I learn that in my weakness
your Son touches me most tenderly.
In my near despair give me
a glimpse of the very martyrdom
you lived in your own life's way.
I pray and offer all up to your Son.
You know your part better
than I can say.

Forgive me when I resent the apparent
ease of your sanctity, and the admiration
of your lovers. I rejoice for you in Him
Who was your Existence. How greatly
you were blessed. Yet your gifts had

their own corresponding crucifixion,
and sometimes I feel a part of that.

\*

O Virgin of Avelino, *aragratiae,*
icon of our family.
Virginity is a dark reality.
You figure it in your gaze.
Byzantine almond eyes and
Hebrew Jewish nose,
icon of our family.
I thank you for who you are
in my life and celebrate
your being. You are a wonder
for us who love you.

Forgive my failings. I really do not
want my life to be this way,
thankless and forgetting of you.
Make our days rich with the memory
and spirit of your Son.
Make our life's travels safe and joyous in Him.
Make us pure in desire and gentle
of heart. May our lives be filled,
through you, with the Love of your Son.

\*

O Virgin of Avelino, our altar
and gateway to Heaven, pray for us.
O Virgin of Avelino, our altar
and place of Peace, pray for us.
O Virgin of Avelino, our altar
and Crucified space, pray for us.
O Virgin of Avelino, our altar
and emissary of Divine Gifts, icon
of our family, never let us go.

# PARAMETERS OF AN EARLIER EXISTENCE

## I.

### 1.

Thinking the vastness conveyed by the word ADVENTURE. Adventure and etched ships with carefully detailed rat-lines and rigging, rows of guns, lines of guns and pennanted mastheads. Adventure with a "Toy of the Month Club" covered wagon or a cardboard frontier fort, a tin castle on a board of green, a little yellow and green tank, lost behind the couch. Adventure in make-believe crucifixions, rescuing Jesus as only an Archangel (Michael, Gabriel or Who?) could with plume and sword.

### 2.

Setting fire to the neighbors' field, who had a saber from Saratoga. Befriending a boy with a cow-skin leather coat and shyness. Tying a friend to an alley fence, accidentally spearing him in the mouth. And tasting dog pee on the backyard rail fence. Burning a doll as Joan of Arc. The shield of the "Black Shield of Falsworth" (*MEN OF IRON*) and a silver sword.

### 3.

Costume party in the mud. Breaking into a basement like storming the Alamo, to steal yards of yellow ribbons. Or crawling along trestles, giving Grandmother's sweater clasp a tiny silver sword and shield with chain to my girlfriend. Books of knights and Greek gods and heroes. And a fine black, handmade helmet from a potato chip can with Mrs. N's costume jewelry for a plume comb.

### 4.

"Authors Cards" of scientists with mops on their heads and philosophers looking like they just stepped from the bath tub.

### 5.

Hiding white mint wafers in an open field to use as Eucharistic bread.

### 6.

Paper castles burning in the living room fireplace. Maps of Robin Hood and play with pitchfork games. Watching Ivanhoe on a white horse and little penances as the TV bleeped. Mrs. F.'s retarded daughter C upstairs in a room full of unused furniture. Mrs. S. who made us laugh when she told us: *"Homer came home,"* and all her little taffeta ball game ribbons.

7.

Tommy Sands and Elvis records. Christ the King Church and Holy Week, the mysterious interior invitation to the lamplighters' fraternity and unsure emotions. R. A. and Robin Hood caps with feathers from her backyard pheasants. Kettle drums and hearing her in the chorale downtown. Sticks for apple bongers. Pricking my fingers to become a "blood brother" with H. N., my father's cousin from Germany. A pup-tent and all-night outings in the jungle of the backyard, five feet from the door step. Bicycles and Indian eagle war bonnets. 2 x 4 swords with wrist guards nailed to last to middle age. Macedonian style capes and short skirts. Gown and robes of white for monk's play and maps showing where the "Monk House" was. Mouseketeer ears and Alamo cars. Coonskin caps. The view of Notre Dame's gold dome from the cornfields.

8.

Drinking root beer for the first time and seeing baby come home. *"Will you still love me?"* Playing doctor with D and N.E.

9.

Visit with Grandma: white apples yellow apples and milk of magnesia. *"A lam belle a lam belle a gitchie gotchie gom belle."* . . .finger games. The Infant of Prague in red velvet before the bedroom mirror.

10.

Bats of plastic hanging from the rectory bannister.

11.

"Namby Pamby" the teacher called me and I thought I committed a mortal sin for looking at the nuns' undergarments hanging inside a wooden enclosure in the backyard of the convent where we were playing Three Musketeers with broomsticks or "Blue Blood the Shunt Pirate" with construction cable spools for guns and ship decks. Egyptian pyramids and raising embarrassing questions of sacramental theology in the 4th grade when someone in the 3rd went to Holy Communion and not caught until it was too late! *"Will he be able to make his FIRST HOLY COMMUNION because it will not really be his first?"* *"Just mind your own business!"* she said.

12.

Sad for breaking my FIRST FRIDAY fast on a potato chip as Mom packed my lunch box or cried running home for reasons I didn't know why and silver foil grotto for Mary's Shrine when someone else came with one of wood or maybe one of the boys had made one.

13.

Indianapolis: First evening in the city. Murat Hotel chandeliers of dragoons' horse hair helmets with leopard-skin bands and braid in the Napoleon Room. Watching "The Turn of the Screw" by Henry James on the TV and taking breakfast at the Tee Pee next night with the B's on College Avenue.

14.

Cottage Dye House. Harry's Laundry. *May-Ying* Laundry. Doctor C's Dentist Office. RCA Repair (Zenith). J's Shoe Shop of the deaf and sign language. UPTOWN Theatre. UPTOWN Drug Store - a man whose son was a Trappist monk at Gethsemani. Buying there my first copy of Augustine's CONFESSIONS in Mentor Edition at the recommendation of Sister M. C. Masonic Building. Murray's Tavern. The American Legion which caught on fire, commanders and bingo games. Watching Saturn with my birthday telescope with M. M. and R. M. Playing school teacher. Boarding House suites and Mrs. S. Barber Shop and Jewelry Shop. St. Joan of Arc crypt and attic above the *baldachino.* 42nd Street Branch Public Library and Mrs. B. "I Could Touch the Sky" written below the telephone poles which looked like electric crucifixes. And laugh like a ninny hyena in the theatre. Playing chess and hearing bicycle wheels exploding in the heart/heat. "Flight of the Bumble Bee" on the piano and the word *taboo* (variant spelling: *tabu*) in Scrabble. "Chess Champ" of College Avenue. Boarding School for make-believe and misspelling must ("most"), to be corrected by my pupils' parents. A marine's blue dress-coat and a neighbor who studied Russian. The Rhumba and Prez Prado. "South Pacific" and the Black Watch Highlanders. Listening to Queen Elizabeth's Coronation speech with one also by Winston Churchill. The soundtrack of the Ceremony of the Keys at London Tower and an argument about the rose as metaphor for woman in "Spanish Harlem."

15.

Shannon's "Roaring Twenties" and the sad-faced ladies of the "Cottage Inn." Up to the Upper Room of SAM'S for Reuben sandwiches and stained-glass partitions (room dividers were of humankind).

16.

St. Elmo's Steak House and the Greyhound Restaurant.

17.
Seeing "The Greatest Story Ever Told" and talk afterwards in a downtown tavern about Max Von Sydow and *"How could his life ever be the same after playing Jesus?".* Going to watch the Cameron Highlanders and the Coldstream Guards, with claymores and kilts and speaking to the Royal Drum Major near the dressing room.

18.
Watching Dickie W. walk down 42nd Street eastward to home as "Walk on the Wild Side," by David Rose and the Orchestra, played through the drugstore speaker in the dusky evening.

19.
Buying Pope John XXIII pictures in magazine at Krogers. Working at Danner's and shy about Barbara D.

20.
Broad Ripple, Indianapolis: KARMA SHOP: buying Nehru shirts and Alan Watt's monograph on Pseudo-Dionysus. PANDORA'S BOX BOUTIQUE: peddling my wall-hangings and getting no remuneration. THE WORD SHOP: buying THE *ZEN* DOCTRINE OF NO MIND by D. T. Suzuki: *"'From the first not a thing is.' . . .this was the proclamation made by Hui-Neng. It is a bomb thrown into the camp of Shen-hsis and his predecessors." [p.22]* and feeling the explosion in my own head twelve-hundred years later. THE MUSIC SHOP: as a high-schooler buying strings and looking at Beach Boy records and pictures of Paul Revere and the Raiders. HOUSE OF CHANG: where lovely Yow-eng works with her parents amidst jade Buddhas and rich silk wall scrolls. Buying brushes and paper, cards and incense and talking about them being Christian instead of Buddhist. Trains and parks. C.Y.O. and swimming contests. THE MOVIE THEATER: watching "LET IT BE" twice, alone because my friend was not free on his birthday three blocks away. The College Avenue Bus. The Central Bus. Restaurants: sipping sodas to lyrics of the Shadows of Knight or Lipton tea. The high school. The mortuary. The canals and the swans.

II.

1.

BEGINNINGS: *"Conceived on a stormy night,"* I like to say, in later retrospectives. *"Straight from the womb, born in confusion!"* Tousled tow-head. Laconic. One soup-bowl size haircut full of disagreement and resentment. Neapolitan ancestry and *Johanniskirke* lineage. Diving morganatic infusions. God fascination and the usual foibles. The same fellow, always, with enough nervous tension for all of Newark and Jersey City. Chinese apples from the Elizabeth Grocery Store and careening car along the Pulaski Skyway at night: a near meeting of a stranger's drunkenness and Death. Windsor knot for Dinky in the Summit Avenue mirror. Carousels and arcades where we played along the Long Branch Boardwalk. Our Lady of Sorrows rectories in Garfield and on Ocean Avenue: crowns with gems for the Infant of Prague and Our Lady of Mount Carmel. [I would make my solemn Profession on her Feast Day in 1983.] Scapulars and rosaries and leather-bound prayer books. Saint Basil's Hymnal. Vigil lights and lace surplices. Bell tower chimes. Ice cream wagon bells and Italian street vendors. Tassels for *birettas* like Mickey Mouse beanies with red-piped ears. Later, THE METAPHYSICAL POERT and THE LIVING TALMUD purchased from the Meadowbrook Mall.

2.

JOHNS HOPKINS, BALTIMORE: Eighteen years of dreadful hospital, off and on. Missing school. Missing family and friends. Missing Life! Tiny bird on window-sill seen against brick wall background, a cardinal I thought, maybe a dull-hued oriole. Others might say: *"Only good for crap on the casement."* I welcome you, my quivering friend." Raj's son. Philipino doctor named Lucretia. Tommy Putnam's minister blessing us both, two boy patients. Baptist and Catholic, long before I knew the phrase, *"Ecumenical Movement."* Baltimore high voltage EKG and the harbor where Mother Seton once waved. Keloids and comfort from the Passionists and a woman named Emma, friendly help from Afro-Americans then called Negroes. Eating in oriental restaurants. No artifice or social barriers: a profound friendship with the "Black" child who had been burned. The *swastikas* carved with black crayons in hospital room coloring books out of my incomprehensible pent-up rage. Transfusions and being the naked object of the examination for medical students, male and female, pulling me in clusters, tugging me awake from my sodium-pentathol sleep. The stone silent Sacred Heart nodding each time we passed. Who says I have an excessive need for privacy?

3.

INDIANA: *Mishawaka* and *Potowatomi Park* in South Bend. *Le Mans Hall* of Saint Mary's and running through Notre Dame cornfields long before the student residence buildings came. Bobbing apples with Holy Cross sisters in fluted headdresses made by my Grandfather. King Ludwig's *Neuschwanstein* coruscating through the Warren Street living room. Dixie Highway and *Hans House Restaurant*. War games along the toll road concrete forms. Indianapolis: Meadows Inn and Meadows Apartments. Doctors' offices, dentists, optometrists and analysts. Glendale Shopping Center. Dalton's. Buying my first Chinese Bible for the beauty of the ideograms. *Camp Rancho Framasa.* Hiding in the roots of a tree by moonlight to escape the torments of the Latin School Seniors. Dropping bread while serving the Archbishop with my guitar-teacher buddy. Holy Communion and Chrism of Confirmation. Receiving the "Charism of Celibacy." Ecclesiastical sinecures and academic posturing. Mixed memories of The Latin School yet eternally grateful for the friends and mentors encountered there.

4.

KENTUCKY: Saint Mary's Seminary, Lebanon. Creek walks with C and TD. Crawdads. Red-bug *Volkswagen* backroad tours while listening to Janis sing "A LITTLE PIECE OF MY HEART" and Steppenwolf scowling "MAGIC CARPET RIDE." White frame church (St. Joseph's) where we sat silent for a while. At the rock quarry we talked of attachments and sex and the pains of our lives. The quarry was then half-filled with water and we had too much seriousness within us. The cost of a burgeoning Christian idealism? Louisville bus trips and meeting with Dad for *shish kabob* at the Marriott Inn. A request signal home by wireless for the brass processional cross, Grandfather's scissors and dictionary [the scissors are in Atlanta, the dictionary in a Monk Cell #7—my room]. Adam's Mod Shop where I bought outfits for the rock band. Seneca Park. Actors' Theatre. Cathedral. The King Fish on the Ohio River. Bellarmine College. Merton Center. November 24, 1971. No room at Gethsemani. Thanksgiving weekend in exile with kind friends. Reading about Maude Peter. Another friend in a red car coat. Learning about silence from the Presbyterians and Saint Paul from the Baptists while staying in their seminaries along Alta Vista Road. And Rod Stewart was singing "REASON TO BELIEVE." First visit to Merton's grave with Dan Walsh, May 1970.

5.

EXCURSIONS WITH THE FAMILY: Passing Sing Sing. Pittsburgh esplanade. The "Spirit of Saint Louis," long before Amtrak. Watching the tail of the train half-circle itself at midnight and lights of industry. Waving to porters in white gloves from our Pullman window. A horror movie, later seen, of hands on the glass and a boy paid a silver dollar not to speak. He kept silent as the hand sank back into nowhere as another adult wasted words with his father. The boy forgot to pick up the silver dollar from the table. A porter pocketed it. Centennial parade at Gettysburg. Being in Boston while a group had a song on the pop charts about the dirty water of the Charles River and courtyards. I had not yet discovered the America Transcendentalists. Instead I was reading *breviaries* in Latin. Canada: Queen Elizabeth Hotel. Cathedral next door and Polish dancers in the plaza below the window where I sat playing a Gibson electric. FDR room. A clandestine purchase of a book on perversions. Coach rides in the park. Cardinal Leger's blessing was that. I had known him from his books. Going to confession to a bilingual priest in lace *cotta*. Peeking in at the dinner for the new Auxiliary Bishop. The Cardinal in simple vestments. Excavations for EXPO. The Fort across the waters, an island filed with soldiers in white leggings and boredom.

6.

EXCURSIONS WITH CLASSMATES AND FRIENDS: High School Senior Class Trip 1966. All twenty-eight of us in a bus, beating Kesey to it by several years. There is a 16mm film of it somewhere. I wore a black riding cap and brown leather jacket in imitation of Bob. Virginia Caverns. Atlantic City: our Rector pleading before we could leave the hotel, *"Who stole the damn ashtrays?"* The half-clad beauties in the bars of New York City and rock bands in imitation animal vests playing "HOUSE OF THE RISING SUN." The Bitter End and advertisements for Neil Diamond, a rising star. Washington Square and O'Henry's Steak House. Not yet knowing Dylan Thomas. Rosie's "Have A Rest" in Niagara Falls. Detroit: staying in the Y.M.C.A. shortly before the race riots. I learned it was fire-bombed after we were there. Place in my mind as I later listened to "Simple Twist of Fate." The great 1969 trip to D.C. with CA and TD on the train boarded in Louisville. Checkered tablecloth, guitar, candle, food. Mountain kids going east joined us. A plaintiff, poignant night of looking back along the dark tracks somewhere in the mountains. Signals in red now and then, signals in green. Anticipating a vision of the "Biscuit of Columbia." We were all in love with Doris. Georgetown Cafes and psychedelic shops with posters of the "Two Virgins," John and Yoko, a scandal in those days. Singing "Walk Right In" during a counter-liturgy in the Little Red Brick Around the Corner Underground Church. Today things are tame by comparison. Museums and the oppression of *rococo* government buildings. Watergate was infamous for being Vatican property. Memphis: again, the Greyhound bus station and the airport, sometimes arriving in the red *Volkswagen*. Guitar in a satchel slung over my shoulder, shirt tails flapping above bell-bottoms. Proud to be welcomed with a kind glance in W.C. Handy Park. Giggles and jiving. To *Barzizzia's* for chairs and *Nehru* jackets. Elvis, of course. Scanning Greek imports of alabaster

Davids, Hectors, Helens, Paris. Was it Athena I chose by my parents? Nashville record shops. Hearing "Lay, Lady, Lay" for the first time, right in the city where it was recorded. Chicago: Picasso's lion in August rain. Waving to President Nixon at the marina. Buying *Zen* books.

7.

NEW YORK: Churches as venues for opera stars. Papal tiara in Saint Patrick's Cathedral later moved to the National Shrine in Washington. Manny's Music Center with pictures of The Rascals on the wall and *sitars* in the window. I could afford some guitar picks, spent my money on photo-documentaries of The Second Vatican Council. Staying in the depressing Chesterfield Hotel and eating cheesecake at midnight. Bob Dylan dreams after buying Daniel Kramer's book in Greenwich Village, the book left behind and reclaimed from a Broadway restaurant where we talked of the coming St. Mary's annual BONFIRE and my new act, nothing to do with 2nd Year Latin or Church History (Lacordaire and Chateaubriand before the First Vatican Council or the Treaty of the Lateran in 1929.) I was afraid to meet the bus alone at the Port Authority. *"You were a native and waited until I departed, my gentle friend."* A silk top hat. A beaver-skin coachman's tall hat a white leather vest and a silver-scaled guitar strap like the one John Lennon used with his *Rickenbacker*.

8.

SOUTHWEST: Moving through Oklahoma like a Kansas tornado. Actual pilgrimages. Roustabout. Tucumcari. Santa Fe: churches as gift shops. Rich artistic ladies. Hand-painted artifacts and leather bridles. Writing a poem in my mind while inside the Cathedral, copying it out on the end sheet of a volume of the *Obras Completas* of Saint John of the Cross. Albuquerque: Olde Town Square. Matadors on restaurant walls, and *ojos de Dios* too. *Nambé* silver and turquoise. *Piñatas* shaped like donkeys. Thunderheads and lightning in the distance. Sidona: hermitages at the Spiritual Life Institute and the mountain chapel. I slept in the car for fear of the "side-winders." Desert birds to wake us. Greeting the day with "How Can I Keep From Singing." Yuma: "Johnny Yuma was a Rebel/he roamed through the West." San Luis, Mexico: dust floors, soft cheese, smiles from the dark girls in the night, fireworks, customs booth and security guards. Return trips East. Bus stop in Winslow as the Eagles sang *"Standin' on a Corner in Winslow, Arizona...Could it be/my Lord!/a girl in a flatbed Ford/slowin' down to take a look at me?...Take it Easy."* Time in stereo. Tears in my ears. Under the glass bubble of the Club Car, Amtrak from California to Emporia, singing "If Not For You" with a pretty girl named Jacki. "Preserve Natural Wildlife Habitat" decal on my guitar case.

9.

CALIFORNIA: Carried to the West Coast whittled down by worry and prayer. Cardiff-by-the Sea and Capistrano swallows. Passing St. Charles Abbey. Pico Rivera, Disneyland, Knotts Berry Farm with bookstore monitors. Spanish flamingoes don't fly in the morning. Grauman's Chinese Theatre (it's name in those days), the Wooden Drum. Denizens of Sunset Strip and drive by the President's birthplace. San Fernando Valley at twilight and Denny's under the half-crescent moon.

10.

VALERYMO: Valerymo Jesus in a loincloth, half *Zuni*, half Spanish Outlaw, strung up on a *joshua* beam. Vocabulary of wilderness, arithmetic of heat, *mesas*, blue pools of light and wood descended by steps to chants in *manzanita* evenings. Chinese block-prints and a wing-shaped *pagoda* on the lake in red. A turtle in the cloister shedding crocodile tears. Father Thaddeus saying, *"If I were a good Zen Master, I would hit you with a stick for your bad calligraphy strokes." "You come from as far away as China!"* Flemish/Belgian accents, pottery and glazing enamels, fires in the kilns, philosophizing in Father Eleutherius's Garden.

11.

SAN FRANCISCO: Electric wire night flight. I set off the alarm, perfect form: little cash, casual clothes, nervous suspect. Is it the spiral notebook or the heavy belt buckle? Dorian Gray's incarnation on a tour to Europe, reading about Napoleon. *"Are you also a megalomaniac?",* I ask straight-faced. Fishing boat lights lie like necklaces on velvet and a bombast of color in the Fourth of July sky, shattering any separation of water and air. Carmel somewhere in the dark below me. Crystal pyramid of the city burns in the night like faggots of glass seen through the drive to their Victorian house guarding Golden Gate Park near Twin Peaks District. A song for Janis Joplin emerges during those days: "Waves of Wah Wah/pedals/over the Golden Gate." *Tatami. Tokonoma.* Persimmons throbbing in a row across a silk scroll while *Bodhisattvas* pointed upward and back down to us. Waitress in *kimono* pours our tea. A visit to the Whitney Museum for Wyeth exposition: "The Nude Lady" of his hidden life. I enjoyed as much the *Bodhisattvas* of cast bronze, a *sumie* scroll painted ever so delicately by finger, whispered words about *Nirvana* and *Samsara* and how they meet in Compassion. Different people doing the same things. *Embarcadero.* Sausalito Ferry. HIGH TIDES BOOKSTORE, mountain chapel, bridge, *Presidio*, Chinatown, North Beach. *Koans* at the Cannery and light lunch in *Ghiradelli Square.*

# TWO *ZEN* MEMORIES

## I. CIMARRON *ZEN* CENTER:  LOS ANGELES, JUNE, 1973

Driving through Santa Anna Freeway through city streets and residential neighborhoods, we at last see the stone enclosure wall and the wooden sign: *ZENJI.* We knock and are not heard. We quietly enter so as not to disturb, arriving at the kitchen door. *"Are you Roshi?"* *"No,"* the young monk answers, with a big smile for the mistaken compliment. *"Have you eaten?"* he asks. *"Yes, thank you, we have."* There is little activity this night at the Center. We take some literature on the programs and schedules of the Center, and accept the invitation to visit the *Zendo.* We sit in the dark room, with single candlelight before the Buddha shrine  My friend is uncomfortable. *"John, I feel like I am in a pagan temple. Are you ready to go?"* My gentle, charismatic friend, so willing to help me find myself, has reached the limits of his own sense of fidelity. We relax with supper at the great restaurant of Chinatown and discuss the meaning of the Trinity during the dark drive home.

## II. THE SAN FRANCISCO *ZEN* CENTER:  PAGE STREET, JULY, 1973

Young American *hondo* in blue *rakusu* that matches his eyes, with close-cropped blonde hair, welcomes us to the Page Street Center. *"Please wait. We will find someone to guide you."* We have arrived unexpected, a bit nervous, not knowing what to expect. *Tai Chi* dancers in the courtyard—silent—strange. A young Jewess with jet-black hair greets us, gracious and soft-spoken.

First room: *rakusu* sewing lesson. The young man sitting across from me is awkward with the needle and silk thread, but smiles. *Namu Amida Butsu—Namu Amida Butsu—Namu Amida Butsu* in and out with the stitchery. The gray-haired lady, wise, serene, says it is good training for men to sew, diminishes false masculine ego. She offers us tea in tiny bowls. *"Oh, you are Catholics! I didn't expect you would be interested."*

Then down to the *Zendo,* practice sitting session, *zafu, zabuton, futon* on wicker matting. *"Please do not step on Buddha's tongue,"* our Jewish guide gently requests. *"We aim to practice respectfulness in all things."* SWAM!: demonstration with the *kyosaku* stick, a thick one for winter when heavy garments are worn, this lighter one fits the season of summer. *"To administer the stick is a painful discipline, especially at first, when you sense your own unworthiness and fear hurting someone else. The more experienced take turns during sitting."* SWAM!: It does not hurt me. I feel the energy rising through my back and neck.

181

Leaving the *Zendo* we meet an older man, close-shaven, with glasses. He is wearing full Japanese dress. I ask about the *kasaya*. *"Yes, I am a full monk but am not into the ordination trip."* We bow and pass.

In the kitchen a bald cook cubes vegetables with a long knife. I discover the cook is a woman—strange. Our guide explains that all are vegetarian, though *"We try to avoid food trips. We all eat the same."*

Next we experience the "Crash Room," for the children of the *Zen* family. There is a place and a room for them. *"Yes, we are a family here."* A young man passes on his way up the steps. He is wearing street clothes. We are told he is the "buyer" for the Center and directs the finances. *"Some of us work within the community, others hold jobs outside and share their income."*

*"Roshi is not here. He is at the Mountain Center. But you may enjoy seeing the Great Buddha Hall where he conducts teachings and ceremonies."* We enter into the vast room, immaculate, radiant with light pouring through the huge Victorian glass arches. Brass bells on silken, stitched cushions, horse-hair *hosso*, exquisite vestments. *"This is the place of making the Bodhisattva Vows and ordination liturgies. Suzuki Roshi's funeral rite was conducted here amid great sadness and joy of heart for him. His spirit is present still."* I find a place of vast silence and, equally, excitation of my imagination.

*Han* sounds and big fish resonators, wooden clappers punctuate the conversation. I ask futuristic questions of our young guide. *"What will you do after this?"* *"I am happy here now,"* she replies. *"Do you have plans for the future?"* *"I am happy to be here at the Center,"* she replies. I want to persist with my questions. My friend catches the meaning of her teaching. We said goodbye to her, briefly visit the Center's Library, full of *sutras* and scrolls, and take back with us back copies of THE WIND BELL.

# CHARLOTTE

Dear Charlotte, I find you gathering
flowers in the Chinese chestnut grove.
Your purple print dress flows to your feet.
Your half-curled hair bobs in the breeze.

We speak of Truth and human choices.
You voice concern for your son and say:
*"It is so wonderful to see him come alive!"*
as he rides by on a borrowed bicycle.

You turn in me the desire to be my best self,
to be a Christian, to know Jesus.
We talk of John of the Cross, and Thérèse's
determination and silent Conchita's
speaking eyes.


# A WALK WITH K

walk with K spiders
red in the sunset, *kudzu*
draped like a green
screen from a MID-SUMMER
NIGHT'S DREAM scene, dragons
giants of ENDYMION
webs taut like bow-strings
Life itself will
help you keep your feet
on the ground.

## SILENCE TO CLARITY

Earth:
the dust settles,
the dew comes up on your brow
at night,
the light comes up in
the morning,
silence to clarity.


## *LA BOTA* (THE BOOT)

Oh, the lovely yellow boot
*la bota amarilla y linda*
perfect for a vase
holder of a delicate rose
in dedication to Salvador Dali


## DISAPPOINTMENT #1

I would not be surprised
if Rimbaud is in Heaven.
But I would be surprised
if he is happy.  Instead,
he is probably making
demonstrations with placards
against the injustice of his
sentence in Eternity.

# THE PORCELAIN *KUAN-YIN*

The porcelain *Kuan-Yin*
in the place of changes
*oremus pro invicem*
needlepoint bracelet
*Rochet*
may I have your permission
to clean out your
former desk
in the
Novitiate?
Thank you
Zorro

# UNDERSTAND

hand stand
head stand
stand
Miles Standish
stand-off-ish
standard
standby
stand off
understand!

# GONE DOWN BAD!

pretty silly
would he feel
witness to a
game gone down
gone down bad!

# THE STREET OF THE FISHING CAT

*Doyene*
*capstan*

The street of the fishing cat

Blue light of heat
your piercing eyes
through incense vapors
your ivory features
your skin of gold illusion
the death of youth
emissary to the beautiful

*Can a man-of-war chase a porpoise?*

Forever set
the voice of stone
forever sung the
sound of peace

By moonlight and laughter
defying all syncophants
camphor incense totally consumed
tears to his ears
melodies to his eyes
a flower of beauty
glowing
in the cold
night of life
bright foil for the dandies
foil to the ladies

You stand inside
his voice
which surrounds you
on every side
up and down
front and back
a fury of mist
a little hat with a glove

in it
you feel hollow inside
but you are not empty

Can you step away from the
Street of the Fishing Cat?

## OCTOBER 16

from your Chinese chestnut
capped stem cream come blasts
carries Life like water
poured over a flower
trickles down
in the desert of your celibacy

through your fox-fur face
bristles anguished pleasure
blasted over the brink
by need and for 'Why's?'
you know not the answer

sleek like river raft
spread dip deep leaf
under the sweet-gum tree
weave fabric of
thought-filled momentous
nothings

sad sound tunes trickle
down chestnut stem
cream come memories
and driftwood woes
thistle hand holders
along the shore line
gold-tone dropping
leaves

crash down oak stands
firewood fences
ripple, dilates, centers
in the sun crushed
stone bench

I dream of you
in tapered flames
brass-wrought morning
I rid my mind of melodies
brought up from solitude


# A PLEA AGAINST THE MIMES

For all the riff-raff who in
their labors groan
For all the saints
For all the salt of the earth
a plea against the mimes

*"How could you ever expect to love*
*with that stewed tomato thing*
*you call your heart?"*

*"The watered-silk night of your*
*black tendencies."*

Genoa sails on boats in San Francisco Bay
The Sausalito fairy wanted to take me home
but I wouldn't let him

*"Walk On!"* cries the cover of a
Christmas Humphreys book.

*impresarios* of religion
masters of evasion
time was
in a kiosk

a clock of need
pristine consciousness of who he
really is, playing imaginary chess
with our feelings

Castration anxiety to equal the fears
of the PIT AND PENDULUM OF POE.

We wear our penis as a badge: Vesuvius,
Rammer, Slammer, resolved of detumescence.

Pigtailed youth, once a Roadie for Harry
Belafonte
now wears bald head, monk's gear, all the pretty
boys are pious

If we met in "Peaches" you'd be the one in
hot pink jeans humming "Knockin' on Heaven's
Door."
I'd be the timid one, somewhere behind the
shelves
reading liner-notes to "Yellow Submarine."


## A PROSTITUTE'S LAMENT

You don't think about it
sometimes
if the man too is
scared
you get a sense of hope
if he is gentle, a start of a
sensation of pleasure
but mostly you are numb
and you do it
you do everything
without thinking about it
without feeling any of it.
They call it *"making love."*

## NOT YOU TOO

There's an imposter going around
he's dangerous cause he looks
just like you but I know he isn't

I know he's not you because you
always have time to listen, you're
always eager for conversation, a walk,
some music

This guy doesn't even have an hour
or catch on when I ask two more times.

On top of all that he's got the gall
to stop me after Compline to do something
for him—repair a book!

It's different with you.

Hope you come back on the scene soon.
This other guy is a constant reminder
of the disappointment of human friendship.

# ONLY LONELY "*GOOD NIGHT*" ONE MORE TIME SAY I

A Dramatic Dialogue in Free Verse

Persons: The Erudite Athlete and the Intellectual Monk
Scene: Holy Spirit Abbey
Time: 1982

\*

## PROLOGUE

The Athlete and the Intellectual--an inner dialogue imaged in others, writers, poets, people of brief meetings, anti-*lectio* reading and wishful thinking. A conversation with myself, a symphony of feelings, a symposium in my imagination. Any resemblance to real people of my life-experience is gratuitous. Thesis and antithesis, wholeness and fragmentation, sexual oneness and celibacy, union with God and alienation from myself. Knowing everything and sensing nothing. Knowing nothing for certain and sensing security. My own needs imaged with others' faces. My face blushed by confusion and the relentless sense of non-accomplishment. A work not yet completed—it is myself.

\*

*"A young girl once stood barefoot on a beach in Normandy, facing the sea and singing. Yeats the poet stood behind her at a distance listening to her song. She sang of the many civilizations that had existed there and had passed away, he tells us. She sang to words of her own, but she ended each verse with the cry 'O Lord, let something remain!'"*

One Japanese skeleton toothless lies dead
dead skeleton toothless poet *Basho*
traveller Japanese poet of splish-splash
memory remembered in late-night
Atlanta conversation: *"I didn't make the
connection."* *Basho* somewhere somehow
met the little baby on the roadside;

*". . .child, you must raise your voice to heaven,
and I must pass on, leaving your behind."*

191

Don't tell me of your life if you can't handle
my own, the urgency of my wanting to be needed.

303 rooms of memories athletes and Sacred *Rota* barristers
meet intellectual obfuscation in my perceptions, more
of possibility than accomplishments:  Greeks, the
Pre-Socratic awareness of their tutorial interest, French
and German for operatic librettos:

*"Ach, mein herzliebes Jesulein*
*Mach die ein rein sanft Bettelein*
*zu ruhn in meines Herzens Schrein*
*dass ich nimmer vergess dein."*

Singers for Services twice on Sundays or
players of volleyball of their own choosing
The great disgusting humiliations of youth
and years it takes to be happy again
a time of grace of promise and
opportunity—trust:

*"Ah, Life! that mystery that no man knows,*
*And all men ask. . .*

But a new form dawned once upon my pain
With grave sad lips, but in the eyes a smile
Of deepest meaning and dawning sweet and slow,

Lightening to service, and no more in vain
I ask of Life *'What art thou?'* as erstwhile,
For since Love holds my hand I seem to know.

*"He makes me swear on a Bible every time he tells me his*
*non-eventualities."*

*"Yes, please come, but only for five minutes."*
Hyper-intense self-concerned athlete wise
man, pilgrim of bicycle-wheeled Europe
and Middle Italian, saving Dante for his
mother-tongues *tertia rima* versifications:

*"...per ch'io te sopra te corono e mitrio..."*

*"Have you tried Goethe?"*

*"Feeling is all:*
*Names are but sound and smoke*
*Befogging heaven's blazes."*

*"or Dylan Thomas lately?"*

*"Dreary me I'd rather be a poet*
*any day and live on guile*
*and beer."*

*"John Donne?"*
*"Seal then this bill of my divorce to all*
*On whom those feigner beams of love did fall."*

*"Arthur Rimbaud?"*

*"At last, O happiness, O reason, I brushed from the*
*sky the azure that is darkness, and I lived—gold*
*spark of pure light. . .I became a fabulous opera. . ."*

*"or Oscar Wilde, actually Irish but most often considered*
*English?"* *"I treated art as the supreme reality and life*
*as a mere mode of fiction. I awoke the imagination*
*of my century so that it created myth and legend*
*around me."*

*"And then there's Yeats, of course, in 1909 Dublin*
*Anthology—soft white Bible paper and green binding,*
*burnished with goldleaf and gold edges."*

Please come back and tell me of your story.
Do you listen to God better than I do?
How are your folks and your family?
I'm here because of my past and the need
for distance. Let us not try to hide the
doubt:

*"'No reason to get excited,' the thief he kindly spoke.*
*'There are many here among us who feel that life is but a*

*joke./But you and I, we've been through that, and this is not*
*our fate,/So let us not talk falsely*
*now, the hour is getting late.'"*

—and can you too say *"sustenance"* without a
misplaced *"b"* while feeling awkward?

*"When you shock me with your sins I'll let you know,"* he said.
*"So what"* says I and flow along like old dead
*Basho* and his allegory of life.  Would he ever
have dreamed he'd turn up in an Atlanta conversation.
No, you did not make the connection,
this time just a second attempt at knowing where
I am with William Butler Yeats of Atlanta.
*"Just tell him, Basho called."*
*"B. o. s?"*
*"No, B. A. S. ho.  Thank you."*

*"Can we believe or disbelieve until we have*
*put our thought into a language wherein we*
*are accustomed to express love and hate and*
*all the shades between?"*

*"Just tell him Basho called."*

No heather no heath no fog-flung
fields of consolation, only distance.  How
silly to sacrifice autonomy, to throw
away solitude care trust confidence for
a newness fireworks fantasy fascination
exclusivity

No volleyball is played during Lent, no
note and noise at least, this morning.
Better to have sung for two Services despite
evening depression and early turning to bed.
*"So it goes, my friend, hope you have someone to*
*confide it to God know the hangers-on seem to be*
*increasing—celibates and misfits*
*orchestrated recluses and High Church ladies,*
*university men and administrators,*
*friends and feelers for affection.  Hold*

*it all in order and remember the little*
*one when you can:*

*"We should not make light of the troubles*
*of children. . .they are worse than ours,*
*because we can see the end of our trouble*
*and they can never see any end."*

*". . .to carry lightly the burden of concern*
*to laugh when feeling lonely,*
*to delight in others when wanting to be together."*

*"So it goes,"* says Kurt.

*"Just watching the river flow,"* says Bob.

*"Only castles burning,"* said Neil.

*"If you hold a person clutched in your hand*
*like sand you will lose him,"* said *Dōgen Zengi*.

And *Basho* shows up in an Atlanta
conversation for guilty reasons and want
of a better accusation—just call it
frenzy, or not—so—quiet desperation—

*"The mass of men lead lives of quite*
*desperation. . .But it is characteristic*
*of wisdom not to do desperate things."*

—or reaching frantically one new time
for a new savior. *URGENT LONGINGS*
easy to read—hard to bear.

Come along and help me pray bless
please don't blow it with fantasies and
possession. Just leave it all behind when
you go to pray alone or if you can
carry it with you to Him and hold it
up with yourself.

*"Here I am Lord not less but nothing more*
*than broken me. So what else is new?"*

Go back to sleep, my new-found friend Yeats
*Basho* somewhere in the distant days
plays rhapsodies on concrete castles
and ice on the pine needles—

*"In this mortal frame of mine which is made*
*of a hundred bones and nine orifices there is*
*something, and this something is called a*
*wind-swept spirit for lack of a better name,*
*for it is much like a thin drapery that is*
*torn and swept away at the slightest stir of*
*the wind."*

You would have come this weekend—

*"I will arise and go now, and go to Innisfree. . .*
*and I shall have some peace there, for peace comes*
*dropping slow. . .*

*I hear lake water lapping with low sounds by the shore;*
*while I stand on the roadway, or on the pavement of grey,*
*I hear it in the deep heart's core."*

—except for the weather—whether, my friend, you
know it or not, the pine trees needed
no one to mirror their ice-needled
beauty. They saw themselves—

*"ancient blade, still as it was,*
*still razor-keen, still like a looking glass*
*unspotted by the centuries."*

—a meadow lark or two came for the
same or just to hear the twigged
tree beat sticks in the recessional
beat of their wings, tipped in white
and black measurements, bellied like
stuffed toys for sale.

Hear the twigged trees beat a rhythm
soft like sticks in simple time, dowels
touching, light like touch touch in the
wind.  You might mistake them for
chopsticks.

But *Basho* is not hungry.  His final
thirst is quenched by rain and the
evading clouds of laughter, the
dripping down of glass bead games
in vesperal entertainment.

*"I walked at full ease scorning the pleasure of*
*riding in a palanquin, and filled my hungry stomach*
*with coarse food, shunning the luxury of meat. . .*
*every turn of the road brought me new thoughts and*
*every sunrise gave me fresh emotions."*

You did not come because of the weather.
If you had you might have sensed all
these things:

*"It pleases me to fancy that when we turn towards*
*the East, in or out of church, we are turning*
*no less to the ancient west and north; the one fragment*
*of pagan Irish philosophy come down, the 'song of*
*Amerigin', seems Asiatic; that a system of thought*
*like that of these books (UPANISHADS), though perhaps*
*less perfectly organised, once overspread the world,*
*as ours today; that our genuflections discover in that*
*East something ancestral in ourselves, can appease*
*a religious instinct that for the first time in our*
*civilisation demands the satisfaction of the whole man."*

Yeats-leaning that you are, you would have plucked
a pine cone and called it a berry cluster. . .

*"I went out to the hazel wood,*
*because a fire was in my head,*
*and cut and peeled a hazel wand,*
*and hooked a berry to a thread. . ."*

And walked out in evening tide to say
goodnight to the day—If you came.

If you be depressed then be fully
who you are if depressed be depressed
and please come back when finished.

Sorry to wake you from your sleep.  You, Yeats,
were not your conversant self.  But I, *Basho,* did
sense a laugh now and then—

*"My joy was great when I encountered anyone with*
*the slightest understanding of artistic elegance."*

Oh, young, silly friend Adonis, Hippolytus or preferably
Yeats, if you wish, hold the sea-shell of
ramifications to your ear and pray
a cart goes by:

*"And then I pressed the shell*
*close to my ear*
*and listened well,*
*and straightway like a bell*

*came low and clear*
*the slow, sad murmur of far distant seas,*
*whipped by an icy breeze*
*upon a shore*
*wind-swept and desolate. . .*

*And then I loosed my ear—Oh, it was sweet*
*to hear a cart go jotting down the street!"*

You suddenly find yourself surrounded
by more hangers-on.  Please don't tell
others I come to speak to you:  *"That*
*is presumed."  "Well, thank you for the*
*reinforcement."*  Instead of Bibles to
swear on we will use one to pray:

*"Dear Jesus, we put ourselves in your
presence, broken as we are, full of
confusion and our own uncertainty."*

Call back some later time if between
5 P.M.—9 A.M. you will get only a
mechanical voice. Please call your local
spiritual director. He is not me. I be
just one more hanger-on. *"Please hang
up the phone when you get the message,"*
said Alan. *"Please get the message before you phone,"*
says you. *"Please
do not phone,"* says I.

Just remember, when you go against
your Spiritual Father's advice you lose.
*"Hello." "I was asleep."* You lost.
*"I'll call you sometime maybe."*
*"Maybe we'll see you before Easter."*

How many times must a man hurt
himself before he gets his own message?

*"Stay free from petty jealousies. Live by
no man's code, and hold your judgment for yourself,
lest you wind up on this road."*

*"Dear Jesus, do you hear my urgent
longings? Dear Jesus, I really am playing
games primarily with myself in this situation."*

No other human being can take away
our aloneness. I can tell you Dunne,
and Hinnebusch, and Tyrrell, page and
line, but I don't' get the message.

*Basho* toothless dead *Basho* once wrapped
in crepe, a hand full with scroll, the
other brushing 古池 蛙 characters across
its surface, cursive script and linked
verse of *waka* and *haiku. Basho,* please
give me 17-syllable remedy for heartbreak.

Dear *Basho,* write one Jesus long poem—

tell him message I am not getting
—long travel to the North Jesus by
Way of *Chuang* and Galilee, *Basho,* to
*Edo* and the Unknown Christ hidden
in chrysanthemum blossom.  Orientals
no stupid eschatologists, all realized
now in fullness, only more Nothing
yet to Hope to see you too.

Dear *connoisseur* of fine experiences please
tell me thrill of first if not mutual
orgasm.  You define not loving in
such experiences as disgusting
humiliation.  Please confirm by personal
conviction for all non-experienced
hangers-on.  Dear arbiter of bitter
indulgences, say more as explication
of how sin builds on nature and

Pre-Reformation analytics.  I decry too easy
identification with the poor.  You
think I do better speaking only in
abstractions.  I feel I give you
*"no stuff"* of myself.  Can I please
tell you of *Basho—un* big *gran*
allegory of life.  Not latinized or
Romanticized but horse-riding
wanderer through *Edo* now Tokyo
experiences.  9 years difference.  I
make good Teacher, huh?  Put
myself out of business quick, huh?

Good old once-dead *Basho* feels his
youth stirred again. When will he
learn?  Better to crawl back in bed *"if
you be depressed"*—but remember words
of wise old *Basho* saying:  *"masturbate
self only make situation worse."*

Good old *Basho* sought finally his
own truth, forgot the frills, threw
away unneeded umbrella and felt the
rain trickle down robe collar like
Cold Mountain *Han Shan's* clear water
allegories. Nature and Man are One.

*"Go to the pine if you want to learn about the pine,*
*or to the bamboo if you want to learn about the bamboo.*
*And in doing so, you will leave your subjective pre-*
*occupation with yourself. Otherwise you impose yourself*
*on the object and do not learn. Your poetry issues of*
*its own accord when you and the object have become one*
*—when you have plunged deep enough into the object to*
*see something like a hidden glimmering there."*

*"Thank you for calling, Basho. It's after*
*8 now and I'll turn back to bed.*
*I'm depressed tonight, Basho, and a*
*bit unknowing of you and us to*
*tell you more, except by the way*
*young novice monk send Atlanta*
*Yeats a poem—HOUND OF HEAVEN."*

*"Oh yes,"* say Basho, "very beautiful
poem young novice monk ask me of
its location."

Dear Old *Basho haiku* replaced by
high lyric poetry.

*"So it goes,"* say Kurt.

*"Just watching the river flow,"* say Bob.

*"Only castles burning,"* says Neil.

Only lonely *"Good Night"* one more
time say I.

EPILOGUE

Athlete dances down steps in the rain
night's companion by the hand
in quick laughter skipping bricks
spends solitary hours with half-hermit
monks on weekends: *"I come for
friendship, not because monks are magical.
There is meeting on shared emotions."*

Intellectual timid monk peers through stained-glass
curiosity, expecting nothing more than
his usual built-in rejection
learns to laugh at himself realizes
his attributes are desireable too.

Yeats and *Basho* exchange bashful verse
talk of limousine ladies, beautiful impossible love
*"Ah women, no intellectual monk or erudite
athlete dancer is safe!"* Heraclitos, God and
madrigals: *"angels of the mists, the lonely
quest, dreams of the unfulfilled and unpossessed,
and sorrow, and Life's immemorial pain."*

mystic rooted in the earth: *"I would parody
your hyper-sensitive verse, Basho, but he
who shoots first must expect to be shot at
in return,"* and spiritual hedonist together
on superb, prodigious undertaking—LIFE
hear equal haunting pleas for permanence in
their souls repeat persistent prayer always
of the same words: *"O Lord, let something remain!"*

and dear old once-dead *Basho* hears Yeats whisper
to some unseen lover:

*"Had I the heaven's embroidered cloths,
Inwrought with golden and silver light,
The blue and the dim and the dark cloths
of night and the light and the half-light,
I would spread the cloths under your feet;
But I being poor have only my dreams;*

202

*I have spread my dreams under your feet;*
*Tread softly because you tread on my dreams."*

—impermanence and relativity—
the attrition of life—What is permanent?

*Basho* and Yeats young silly zealous reincarnations
of poets past and everyone's dilemma recall to mind threefold promise of Jewish-Hellenistic Paul:  faith, hope, love!
yet feel their faith wax and wane, hold in heart hopes
shattered, love misdirected, rejected or somehow unrequited

always knowing purgation, desire it to be positive,
a *'purification'* leading somewhere

young Adonis runner and sagacious forest dweller
dream and yet try to keep their reasons level
hold fast to ideals and beg to hold themselves and
all others in mercy for their failings

—all the paradoxes of this troubled existence—

*"There is nothing that is not religious, you would*
*put it, Basho,"* says Yeats.

*"Ah yes, friend Yeats, old Basho knows simple true*
*Zen saying:*

*'Sitting quietly, doing nothing, Spring came!'*

and so too in our lives, as Jesus said in the parable:  *'The*
*wheat grows of itself.'*  All good things in their own time."

## SO MINE IS A LIFE

So mine is a life
of great contrasts:
a large, blank white canvas with
occasional splotches
of color
here and there

*Zen* saying:
see
that
colors and white
are the same!


## A SELECTION OF VERSE FOR MY FATHER
## ON HIS BIRTHDAY

A part of me
and as much, I guess,
somehow,
a part of you too
is contained in this book.
You not only gave
me life
and the example of
discipline to write,
a desire for good work
of the mind,
a reverence for words,
but, typically, the book and pen for
these poems.

# BORROWED WISDOM

### 1. WINGS OF LAW AND SPIRIT

There is a pigeon with a wounded wing in the cloister. In his Chapter talk on Sunday, Reverend Father used it as a metaphor to our spiritual lives: there is the wing of Law and the wing of the Spirit, when one is wounded we cannot fly.

### 2. JASON THE FIRE-TRIED/SAVED CAT

Jason the fire-tried/saved cat (and a copy of SELF-ABANDONMENT, charred) returns from his not-so-trappist nightly rounds scratched and scarred and bleary-eyed and dissipated and consumed by *ennui.*

### 3. SO, YOU ARE SITTING THERE IN THIS DUSKY MORNING!

So, you are sitting there, in this dusky morning, in the corner of your intellectualism! *"Please don't abandon me to that fate." "Take the journey from your mind to your heart." "I hope he gives you about 20 years." "Maybe we never accomplish it until death."*


# THE LONESOME LAWYER

1.
Heavy drinking
hard living
work was a *"ghost town"* today
and I was thinking about
God for some odd reason
and all that energy
gone to Nautilus and
*haute cuisine.*

2.
You,
in your three-piece
pin-striped suit your $40,000 job
your fast cars
and your

fancy ladies
and your misery
you come to me
for pity.


## THERE IS NOTHING THAT IS NOT RELIGIOUS

The haunting plea for permanence
I hear it in my own soul;
how often I've prayed the same prayer.
Impermanence and relativity;
the attrition of life; what is permanent?
Saint Paul tells us three things last:  faith, hope, love
Yet we feel our faith wax and wane,
our hopes shattered,
our love misdirected, rejected or somehow
unrequited.
Always a purgation, and hopefully,
a positive purification.
To dream and yet to be realistic;
not to give up on our ideals
but still to have compassion on ourselves and others for not
meeting them.  To go beyond ourselves
and to accept ourselves:
all the paradoxes of our troubled existence.
There is nothing that is not religious.
As the *Zen* saying has it:
*"Sitting quietly, doing nothing, Spring came!"*
So too in our lives as Jesus said in the parable:
*"the wheat grows of itself."*
All good things in their own time.

# ALL GOOD THINGS IN THEIR OWN TIME

MARK 4:26-29

Superb, prodigious undertaking—LIFE
and equal haunting plea:
*"Oh Lord, let something remain!"*
Paul's threefold promise:  faith,
hope, love;
yet we feel our faith wax and wane,
hold in heart hopes shattered and
love not returned.
Knowing attrition, we pray it
be *"purification leading somewhere."*
Dreaming, we try to keep our
reasons level; holding fast to ideals
we beg ourselves and others mercy
for our feelings
*"There is nothing that is not religious,"*
we come to say.  And so, in us, as Jesus
in the parable said:  *"the wheat grows
of itself."*  All good things in their own
time.


# STILL CHEWING *KOAN* "LIFE"

grade school stretching to light Solemn High Mass candles; losing tennis balls
to roof; climbing church attic; learning *"Ecumenical";* mind-body booming with
alchemy of adolescence; knowing proximity "Hard Rain," Beatles, Vietnam,
assassination—'71 resident seminarian golden Buddha on *Summa* throne; incense;
Chinese; 50th Anniversary banner, kaleidoscope carpet; kids; old folks; "Folk
Masses"; Berrigans; shifting *Curè d' Ars* to Merton *Zen* in search of something
I knew not what—now grateful looking back with you from Trappist solitude;
still chewing *koan* "LIFE"; still trying to yes myself and others into being and
love; still trying to answer Jesus' call—*"Follow Me."*

# AFTER LAUDS

misty
cloister
swallow
on rock
fluidity &
solidity


# ANGELUS ON WHEELS

sitar strains
*chikari* strings drone
as the sun sets
aureola of gold
the ducks come
white swan
on main strings
for tuning pitch
*suranji* memories
brown robed Franciscans
Trappists in
black & white


# THE RE-EDUCATION OF A TIMID MONK

after the concert, what?
after the ride home, what?

education/re-education/seduction
of a timid monk

Jesus speaks to me these words:
*"Si oculus tuus simplex est..."*

simple
clear vision
unity of purpose
determination of will

write from memory once again essay
on friendship as *"light switch"*


## *"THERE'RE MORE SONGS ON THAT ALBUM"*

1.
You in your white overalls with their "If I had a
Hammer" loop
gimp cavalier in plaid pants and your hands in
your pockets
for first petition.

2.
You, the knower of the silken-satin care of a
woman's love
and only God can satisfy your sensitive heart
how you considerably cried in your Novice
Master's presence
consequent to your tear-eyed laughter
tight-wound like a snare drum
strings vibrate when you walk

3.
Dear *"Misha* Junior:" Now that your muscles have
relaxed
you can do the *durango conmigo* too?

Dear *"Pockets:"* I would like to put you in mine
and take
you home.  Love, Jesus

Dear *"Left-field:"* Don't worry about being so far
removed.
When you're that far out you become the center
of attention.

4.

Get out of the way, kid,
make your room the vastness of God
build it deep with a window of grace
and a doorway to others in compassion

5.

Sitting in a tree, chickens cackle in the
blacks' back yards
looking out a window
playing the same track (on the record) over and
over and
over again

6.

*"There're more songs on that album!"*


## BOB DYLAN: "THE AMERICAN *VILLON*"

Bob Dylan
undercover outlaw
in grey-felt sky
and canvas kickers

\*


Few figures in our folklore compare:
Paul Revere, Billy the Kid.
Thomas Merton called him
*"The American Villon",* perhaps
implying the religious anti-hero.
Whatever designation you choose,
you have to grapple with him.
To grapple with him is to grapple
with your own feelings, your
own self.
That is his project and achievement.
Our task is to detail it.

# GREEN MORNING MOTH

green morning moth
good morning little friend
there's more to life than you know
wake up little friend
there's more to life than you know
do lovers always wake smiling from their
wedding beds?
morning moth—distant hill
humming bird—tree and roots
full-harmony of all things

# SOLEMN PROFESSION

## JULY 7, 1983 - DECEMBER, 1995

## *ZAZEN*

Counting breaths to the crescendo of the wind
inhaling with the breeze
earth *zafu* wind *rakusu* tripping *kyosaku* stick.

Sitting upright.

This time NO ONE sees
*Buddha* sits not beside me but me
and Jesus laughs through the trees
a monist lullaby.

# SOLEMN PROFESSION RETREAT

1.
These sounds are so familiar
and foreign for their settings
felt-layered rows of trees
verdant and golden orb of oil
movie sets and breezes from
a distant location

the countless gifts the great gift
of life and freedom
not in magnitude but seen
in windows of hay
rows of wheat-sheaf splendor
poetic patterns of walks at sunset

Compline bell tolling
bell tower towering the crest

no fear no aloneness this time
just simple nothing-happening *zazen* evening
counting breaths to the crescendo of the wind
inhaling with the breeze
earth *zafu*
wind *rakusu*
tripping *kyosaku* stick

to have no consternation
to have no gauntlet to fling
to have no upset or argument with God
to gently lay aside preoccupations of ceremony and
sociability
to think of her and him and them
to remember, to forgive, to ponder
to wonder where, not why

2.
I spent my first day slowing down
*zazen* effort and contortions
3 days working through the emotions
of not being needed.

3.

Having no set schedule I sleep when I am tired, read,
walk in the exquisite beauty of these evenings, alone, so much
like the lush imagery of Donovan's songs, sit in *zazen* meditation,
pray, do nothing, go to 4:15 A.M. Mass.

4.

Friday Evening
creek near St. Maurus field
glass ripple green circlets and yellow
flies and feathered movement simple light
shines through leaves no serpents but
in fantasy. Jesus shining through *Buddha* nature
bathed in grace *rakusu* robe stole suspended
on shoulders of ease after running from
imaginary snakes in the waist-high grass
to recapture former hierophanies
Our Lady of *Einsiedeln* emerges in written words
and memories her feast too to collide with
personal delight and sad reminiscences
having sat here many times before I sit alone
how to deepen the search for God—stop trying
how to love him more—let self be loved by Him
only with stain on paper and green bindings of
medieval book—to make such a fuss—we all
do it, and pass quietly and quickly away.

5.

IMAGES OF SAINT MEINRAD—every word written with the
blood of immaturity, every line with the knowledge of change.

6.

The prism that sheens is water
a stream a rivulet wreathed with
bowers, vines, branches wrapped with
spider filaments, midge streaks and
summer streamers fresh green from
rain last fallen
shimmer glass-like orbs of refraction
dips and curves or riplets amber in the
peeking sun-filled porous droplets
diaphanous hour, thick, meshed time of

Nature's silencing and memories flowing
in and through and beyond mind's sight
fragile petals, frail leaves floating in and out
of awareness, an effort to recapture, glimpse again
O, let it go!  others will come in their turn and
time.

7.
sitting upright like a *Buddhist* monk
just like in the pictures
this time NO ONE sees
*Buddha* sits not beside me but me
and Jesus laughs through the trees
a monist lullaby, no contention
space the speculations just sit and enjoy.


## FALSE HOPE

If they had a
night together.
they wouldn't be
satisfied.
Their bodies
would invent
10 different
ways
to want each other.


## MAN IN A GABARDINE SUIT

There's a man in a gabardine suit
he's young and he is so cute
and he's looking for you.

# ATLANTA:  A SATIRE IN UNEVEN OCTETS

1.

In buildings with portfolios
leaders meet hierarchs of defiance
lurking with quilted grimaces in copybook unbalance
corniced smiles of reprisal for expenditures
of interest and remunerated energies
ledgered affidavits
architectural fallacies of imagination
situations of their syntax undissolved grammatical abstractions

2.

In offices with 3-piece suits
executives face mediators of finance
perfumed renegades from household honesty
puffed up in their pleated whispers
silver-plated utterances
conspicuous bigots of form, felons with
clock-safe locks of white-washed regret
*facades* of undisclosed mathematics

3.

In barracks with *epaulettes*
brigadiers salute mappers of destruction
reactor chroniclers to the ringing of the blade bell
counterfeit regimental violent redefinitions
superfluities of speech through esophagus triangular
verbal regurgitations misguided fleets of non-suspension
inflammatory plumes of spite
missiles of resentment left unattended

4.

In ballrooms with corsages dreamers kiss their
mates ladies of dark acquisition silk blouses
involuntary perusals obligatory matches
flare from their fantasies and futuristic eyelashes
*Yes* shaped to the tyranny of the situation
unresolved syntax mannequins for the fashion industry
polyvalent karats combed with platinum bracelets
monogrammed nightmares of reactionary splendor

5.

In gymnasiums with sweat socks
athletes tumble models of Adonis in terrycloth
puerile Venus complexities of mood wrestle
politico butterfly bolts from cash belts of check
renumbered chapters with suspenders
paupers of the mind hiding behind *facades* of
chrome strapped to the tune of multiplication routines
elastic lines of refinement and mechanical intimates


6.

In concert halls with flat-wound strings
silver speckled mimes remind of megabucks and
amplitudes of juice blues regenerate diction
geometric sound of corridors and confidence men
fuschia floppy discs mathematical calculations
tell-tale Eucalyptus triangles Darwinian jews-harps
and wind-shield flappers cursing through the
blistering precision of bathos


7.

In airplanes over monasteries and churches arcane ritualists
bless in capes of timeless brilliance greet the morning watch
with post-victorian persuasions and sideward smiles
transcendental mascots and ski-borne mystics slide along
their ancient rulers verbal and symbolic juxtapositions
syntactical rubrics Hellenistic reminiscences and apostolic
testimonies to the trumpeting of psycho-political factions
alibis for carnage in the alleyways catastrophes for
   innocence.


8.

Atlanta-buildings with portfolios offices with 3-piece suits
   barracks
with *epaulettes* ballrooms with corsages gymnasiums with
   sweat socks concert
halls with flat-wound strings airplanes over monasteries and
   church leaders
and hierarchs executives and mediators brigadiers and
   mappers and dreamers and
mates terry cloth athletes and silver speckled mimes arcane
   ritualists undissolved

grammatical abstractions undisclosed mathematics missiles
   of resentment left
unattended monogrammed nightmares of reactionary
   splendor mechanical intimates
blistering precision of bathos catastrophes for innocence—US!

# "MODELS OF NARCISSUS"

Alibis of nightmare and seven-storey pillows
Missionary Union women meet single gender
liaisons
rendering male superior position obsolete
mustached inhabitors and slipping naked
reminiscences
Victorian treacheries of exasperation
Religion and psychological insights
male inferior backward positions and penile
Hellenistic apostolic testifications
a turn of the head a reassurance
man of night-time brilliance greeting morning
watch
Anabaptist persuasions premature prelates from
Sodom and Gomorrah beds stood upright
in hidden closetways total exposed nightmare
Mr. Omnibus capes on the night-flier fiction
verbal juxtaposition. Pennsylvania toothpick
rapist poinsettias. In department stores with
corsets and polyester models meet.


# CHICKAMAUGA CREEK

fog in and out
frost and sheer pine cliffs
contrasting frost with stone
streamers of ice here, there


# SUNDOWN OVER NASHVILLE

WKDA train trestles
tall buildings not here in 1974
pastels and smog
Loretta Lynn and low income housing

# GRAVE OF THOMAS MERTON #2

Merton's grave
snow falling
straw wreath
wind


# AFTER NIGHT OFFICE

*Sesshu* patterns
in the woodblock floor
*"It is our special joy*
*to be nothing and to*
*know that God is All."*

Merton
chanting holding notes
and letting go ideas
sleep and memories drift
away to acceptance and
sense of familiarity

more of a *Zen* experience than
expected when opening
Chapter Room door for short cut
to Cloister
monks sitting in meditation
deep *pranyama* breathing

.

## EYES AND EARS FULL

Eyes and ears full
hands heavy with books
heart warmed
feet on familiar and new
places
nose teased by cheese
and pine, incense and silage


## GRAVE OF THOMAS MERTON #3

Merton's grave
crunch of snow
under foot
white flakes on
wreath red ribboned
bark of dogs east morning pigeons
crown of thorns?
Christmas garland?
Incarnation.
Am I striving for an effect?
Be, be here, be still
yet pencil and paper
in hand to capture it
and the dogs bark still

## ALL YOU CREATORS

the potter, the painter
the iconographer
the lover, the singer
the guitarist, the hesychast
the calligrapher, the luthier
the actor, the redactor
the orator, the flutist
the florist, the chemist
all you creators
praise the Lord


## GRAVE OF THOMAS MERTON #4

Merton's grave: For all this time
I've been looking in the wrong
place, standing in the wrong
direction. The name plate on
the cross faces away from the
grave. Perhaps the cross is
at the feet, not the head,
or behind the head facing
away.

Wet grass. Drops of rain on
the cross. Wet—but now
cars on Highway 247—in some
way less removed than Holy
Spirit from Highway 212. The
world goes its way. A crow
calls. Rain drops on cement
steps near the bell tower.
Thick, gray clouds, dark wet
trees.

# UPPER LEVEL GARDEN

Upper level garden behind cemetery
Statue of the Sacred Heart:  silent
sentinel against leaded
sky, positioned visual
in valley of two distant
knobs.  Hands in *orans* and
gentle protection.


# THOMAS MERTON'S *ZEN* GARDEN

Merton's *Zen* garden:
rain patter on stone and flesh.
Merton is teaching me
to be myself.
Nothing spectacular is
happening.  Just me!


# *LOURDES* GROTTO IN THE RAIN

*Lourdes* Grotto in the rain
and packed-leaves path
retention wall like a fortress
with guns or ancient war ship
simple plaster statues
greened with fungus
and rain


# THE TALE OF TATTERED LEAVES

Thinking of Merton's garden.
What does the tale of
tattered leaves tell
of him, of then, of now?

## FUJIS ON THE HORIZON

Vast bolts of unravelled
grey blue (clouds of cloth) fog,
embossed on green
pine tree pattern

the hoot owl has gone away
the trees advance one by one
from their nighttime hiding

light plays on power lines
paints *Fujis* on the horizon


## PATH EAST OF HERMITAGE

Rich thick cedar forest
path east of hermitage
arching toward Abbey
behind and beyond
Brother Donald's hermitage
marshy ground rivulets
of water sparkling in mossy
mushy mats, facing directly
into the sun just above
the tree lines framed by the
water tower, right, bell tower,
left
splashing through, corduroys
held high up with a hand
at each side.  I come upon
a spring, at this point c. 4'
wide, shallow, stepping-stones
trickling the water down.

Soothing sound of water in
counterpoint to some motor
running somewhere, left, moon
behind me and still boom
and shake of guns now knob with fire tower

straight ahead, path veering to
the left where power lines
intersect sky and land,
Abbey now to my back, my
shadow in front of me as
I turn 45 degrees right where power
line pole is.

Being alone, even apart from a
Community I am visiting my head
is full of what to say to my own
brothers at Conyers, how to convey
what I've experienced without being
misunderstood, and worse, misquoted.
Some are constantly looking for contrasts
and would use words to justify
their own ideas. And what would
be my purpose?

A full concentration of trees, green and
gray, a concentration of light shining
through to the underside of a
broken branch.


## *DHARMAKAYA:* WORKING ON TRUE NATURE

working on inner nature
looking up seeing clouds
awakening ears
hearing sighs


## *LOGRAIRE* INVITATORY

After *Terce*
Merton's grave
wet ground
car whish
woodpecker

*Lograire* invitatory
crow call
water patter
cow moo
cold feet
meadow lark
waking up

hope of
resurrection
signed by
this man's death

## SHADOWS IN THE *ZEN* ROOM

shadows in the *Zen* room
dim lights flickering
movement of monks whispers
books ancient carried
wrapped in cowls
*incognito* and
recognitions

## KENTUCKY *ZEN*

On the winds,
wings of *mantra*,
sacred word,
prayer word.

Feel his absence.
Know his presence.

There are five *zafus*
in the Chapter Room.

## KENTUCKY ARTS CENTER

glass, chrome
purple carpets
snow, river


## SIGNS FOR ST. MEINRAD

images—"*St. Meinrad 8 Miles*"
majestic sun disk
seeking its view
through clouds
snow cliffs
seen against it


## THOUGHTS OF THE MERTON CENTER

Thoughts of the Merton Center.
trying to sort all that out
a poem comes. . .

Golden Buddha
in a room of books
I had forgotten
your beauty.

# WHAT TRACES DO WE LEAVE?: A POEM IN PROSE

*"Time flies faster than an arrow; life is more transient than the dew. No matter how skillful you may be, it is impossible to bring back even a single day of the past."* Zen Master *Dogen*

\*

Counting the chimes of the midnight clock. Thoughts like *zen*-dust fall on a mirror of air. Memories in demanded recognition fall one by one into prayer. Falling. Falling. Nowhere to alight. *"Glad you are here!"*, the monk Guestmaster said. Where is *here*? What is *here*? Returned past? Renewed acquaintances? Prayers one by one fall like dust into a void of meaning. You cannot put it into words. You cannot explain it to yourself. The past and the present remain the same, just the same. The past ever falling into present reality. The chimes, mellow in the night, cadence the night, create sound sequences—intermittencies grace and light—sin and darkness—sorrow and aspirations. Are you *here?* Can you be more *here* if you try?

I pace the Archabbey Church, while in Cistercian hooded cowl, silent ghost to my past, momentary incarnation in a familiar place of someone who is no longer here. Reclaiming pain and joy, hearing inner voices of people not seen in a decade of years. Reclaiming carpet and concrete, marble and wood, the veiled tabernacle, the DeWitt *"CHRISTUS,"* the *Einsiedeln* Madonna. Reclaiming, acclaiming and letting go. Many things now transposed. A new Archabbey on the opposite side. Humanness and brokenness, fragility and nobility of purpose. Shifting situations and buildings of stone. Paradigm of monasticism itself: ancient heritage always transcending the material order.

A ship of glass and sandstone, Saint Meinrad sails along an hourglass sea. A mass of steel and concrete, it dips in the waves of time. Sail on brass bright vessel. Glide with the clock tower cadence of your cracked ship's bell through the bright black night.

\*

*"The flowers that are like brocade on the spring mountain will scatter and be carried away without trace by the stream."* Zen Poet *Dairyu*

\*

What traces do we leave? What remains of us in the lives and places of others after we are gone? Are there traces of me here? Yes and no, I answer to my own question. The deep emotions, the defeats and quiet triumphs of a student remain hidden in his past. The young monks here now know nothing of me nor their seniors' goodness to me along my way. I am a guest in their home, object of curiosity for a brief while. The young students here now know nothing of me nor their teachers' encouragement along my way. What can I tell all of them of Saint Meinrad's meaning in my life, and how it seems someone died when I left. I walk, carving new traces to vanish when I leave. The old is made new. What is over is by grace recreated. Extinguishing footprints. Walking near the parish church. The county bank. The Shady Inn. The Modern Store. The Post Office and Vaal's Grocery. Twin Lakes and Saint Joseph's Shrine. In Conley Hall a Memphis student does not know the memories of me and others confined by the walls of his room. Brothers' Paradise and Saint Jude's Guesthouse. In Sherwood Hall new theologians stay in rooms I used—*fora* where Von Balthasar and Bonhoeffer, Merton and Wilde and Thoreau and Berrigans all met in the mystery of human ideas. The name of another priest on a well-remembered office door. The Icon Shop. The Scholar Shop.

Under the "bubble" of Benet Hall I face out from below the glass. Music blares as collegians talk. The melodies are not unlike our own, perhaps a Springsteen instead of Dylan. These students and I are strangers to each other. They do not know they are in my room of fourteen years ago. In this corridor spirits whisper, some shriek. Where are all our classmates now? To my left the room used by companion since high school days, now no longer a priest. What did we really feel while we were here? What did we really know about ourselves during those days?

\*

*"There is no place to seek the mind; it is like the footprints of the birds in the sky."* The *ZENRIN*

\*

I cross the open field and up the hill of the Stations where I used to read the texts of *TAO* and reveled in the unintended pun of "Theology Activities Organization." Ahead now, the monastery cemetery. Christ cold dead on a concrete cross, surrounded by a retention wall of stone. I stand behind the "Unstable" built as a gift of gratitude by our college graduation class. Now I pass the road wedge where the once freshly planted sapling now stands a tree.

I sit in Bede Hall Practice Room 5, a favored hideaway. Next door an unseen but heard pianist plays *arpeggios,* stiff and hesitant. Outside on the turret with its 360 degree view, the early morning sun warms my face and hands. A solitary truck rolls along the north/south road. A stillness in the air after the movement of years. Under the pine grove trees near Our Lady's Grotto the morning dew lays secure from the heat. Elsewhere, rock and earth manifest their original faces. A white van like a tiny toy pulls away from the Packing Plant. Now eye-level with the spires of the Archabbey church, century old sentinels, sometimes oppressive defenders, sometimes Chanticleer to the goodness of life itself, sometimes glorious herald to Resurrection's hope. I choose the last as my mood and go inside to escape the wind.

In the stillness of the morning I sit in a room formerly the apartment of my President Rector. A window opens east. From above the distant tree-topped hills the sun casts light across the farm fields. A creek trickles below an unsteady bridge barely seen. Corn stalks and wheat sheaves line like regiments across splotches of amber, imagined aggressors with bayonets extended turn slowly into a parable of peace. In this room now a simple chapel, I sit and enter my mind.

\*

*"When the disciple's insight is identical with that of the master, the master's power is diminished by half. When the disciple's insight surpasses that of the master, then he is worthy of receiving the transmission ."* Master *Hyahugo* '*Ekai*'

\*

In 1337 cloistered Emperor *Hanazono* founded a shrine which he called "Temple of the Marvelous Mind." Is there a "different mind" here at Saint Meinrad than my own mind? What is transmitted by Saint Meinrad to those who come here for a while? Is it something outside of books, not expressed in words? Some kind of seeing into our own natures? An arrival at some type of inner freedom? My mind wishes to attach to nothing here. I visit haunts old and hallways just discovered and I pass away. Yet my mind is my mind for having been here, then and now. I have no need to hold on to anything here. What is really here has already been given to me.

\*

Seeing reality as it is. Letting go of idealization, images and perceptions fabricated out of need. This is master's desire for maturing student. Good teachers need good students. This is the pivot of all true learning. The transmission of mind by mind, mind to mind, the fusion of minds demands it. Truths demanded more than truths taught. Minds open to minds giving. Saint Meinrad masters, men and women to Christ committed, give what remains with us when we go. The transaction total, the transmission complete. At one with our own natures, we know the key to seeing what is to be seen, to acceptance of reality, of particularity of vocation, is within ourselves.

## TWO MOONS OF MARCH

1.
The moon,
a silken theater mask,
ashen wit
tragedy, its diamond ribbands,
two rows
of stars.

2.
The moon,
the bamboo flute
the love,
the pain.
Yes!


## RETURNING FROM ATLANTA

rich red wet clay
gashes in the earth
rain purple asters
and dogwood
petals flattened by
the rain
yellow and amber
branches brightening
the road side

the weathered barn
the vast Japanese vistas
of rain-soaked pines
hills and mist

## SWEET DENISE

Sweet Denise,
I'd show you myself
if I knew you'd
know how to really
show yourself to me.


## AFTER BEING ASKED FOR MY "BROTHER'S" BLESSING

I was not able
to speak a word
to that request
the silence and the gesture
were all I could give
and the intent
of my heart
for your good

# THE SACKING OF 16 TITE STREET, LONDON:
# 24 APRIL 1895

Christians, they crashed down the doors of the infidel. Crusaders,
they sacked the shrine of genius and family innocence. Their mood, blazing
righteousness, their stance, *"See what he's done!"* *VOX POPULI*

With Holy Gospel in attendance and armed escorts of the Law,
they looted. Up walkways of travertine, along sage-green walled
corridors, believers and bribers, they battered and shattered with
tainted curiosity. *RES GENTES*

Through flaming peacock passageways, past porphyry Adonis
pedestalled, they pushed and rushed to where, they thought, each
next beautiful mesmerizing Sphinx once did slink to fever his
imagination. *"See what he's become!"* *VOX POPULI*

Cyril's knights and little Vyvyan's castles crafted of child's dreams
turned auction blocks and dungeons of boyhood's horror in one
lewd touch. Iron bolts bar nothing when locks to alabaster hearts
lie rent. *RES GENTES*

*Éditions de luxe* and love letters to Constance in a leather case of
blue, yellow books of prose and verse inscribed, *"From the Author
to His Bride," "From a Poet to a Poem,"* taken. *"He's no right to
privacy now!"* *VOX POPULI*

At 16 Tite Street, they brawled and they bartered, they clattered
and shattered until Chelsea's sad sun sank wet under webbed
silhouettes of Royal Albert Bridge. *"He must go in disgrace,
and far from the crown!"* *RES GENTES   VOX POPULI*

\*


From 16 Tite Street to Reading Gaol, from *Dieppe* to *Berneval-sur-
Mer, Posilippo* to the Alps to Paris, they pressed him with brandished
bigotry. Orange Dublin would not have him alive, nor Golden
Oxford. Scarlet Rome, only as he died.

\*

236

*"Do you realize now what Hate blinding a person is?"* Morality's
outcast asked. *"An Atrophy destructive of everything but itself,"*
his remembrance of '95. Christians, keep this Anniversary!

*RES GENTES   VOX POPULI   DE PROFUNDIS*

237

# PRINCIPLES AND PRACTICES CONCERNING CONTEMPLATIVE FORMATION

Serious work has been going on among us Cistercians of the Strict Observance. Everyone is involved in some way. Democracy, while not the foundation of our Order, is the order of the day. Distressing news has been coming from all sectors of the contemplative world: "SYMPOSIA EXHAUST CISTERCIAN SPIRITS!" "COMMITTEE SESSIONS WEAKEN TRAPPIST CONSTITUTIONS!" "ALL-NIGHT VIGILS BEFORE FLICKERING SCREENS!" And we the heirs of a literary tradition unsurpassed in form and content will transit "EG" and "LC" and "CoCo." Such dreadful logographs show the strain on our electronic scriveners. They are prostrate in front of their machines. Such assaults on our linguistic sensibilities must not harden us. The reports of the GENERAL CHAPTER will be arriving soon. The CONSTITUTIONS are still to be finalized. There is an impending NOVICE DIRECTORS' MEETING. The following lines and lessons, for the benefit of the novices, are being offered to all of us professed who needing them the most hopefully will not profit from them the least.

\*

The first duty in the contemplative life is to do nothing as much as possible. The second duty is to refuse to explain why.

Religion in the world is a virtue that expands, in the monastery a vice that constricts.

The supreme risk of the religious life is righteousness. Without doubt there is no faith in the monastery.

Truth is in harmony with itself. All discord comes from seekers of Truth.

In the monastery that which is most considered is of least importance, that which is most important most obvious.

The monastery is the meeting place of the over-experienced and the under-experienced. The novice is both at once.

Culture and well-breeding and education are absolutely essential before one enters the monastery. In the monastery they have not yet been discovered.

Those who leave their bodies in the world lose their souls. Nothing spiritual is realized except through the senses.

To deny the senses is to elude oneself. Not to deny the senses is to elude oneself.

In the monastery ignorance is a plot, innocence a ploy.

Knowledge is gained at the loss of knowledge. Self-knowledge is the beginning and the end of contemplative life. The end of the monastic life is justification for its meanness.

The most interesting aspect of a religious is the habit: it is both a veil and a manifestation.

The novice who is seen is not conspicuous

The novice's intelligence, like the novice's virtue, is kept well hidden.

Humility is the mark of those who esteem themselves. Those who despise themselves will be humiliated. Those who despise others hate themselves.

The vow of poverty is the substitute for care, the vow of chastity care for substitutes.

Of the vow of obedience more is heard than read. Only those going somewhere keep the vow of stability. Those going nowhere go there.

In the monastery the unwritten rules, the non-appointed rule. All else is a pretext.

One ultimately is one's only superior. All other control the superior has is a deception. Only the powerless truly govern. To lead the monastic life is a rare thing indeed. Most follow.

Those who have no disciples are the best spiritual directors.

The hardest penances are not chosen.

Solitude is the highest form of compliment to oneself, the noblest service of others. Only the solitary loves enemies. Only the solitary is loved by friends.

Correspondence with oneself is consolation for the thoughtlessness of others.

Visitors are a revival for the tranquil, a circus for the restless.

Silence is the abode of the enlightened, the bedlam of the inane.

Words are flowers from the garden of the deep, gongs from the belfry of the dull.

Only the one who has something to say is silent. Only the one who is silent speaks the truth.

Speaking is the medium of those who have something to say, signs and notes the mode of those who have something not to say.

It is better not to speak and be misunderstood than to speak and be understood. To tell all is to lose one's fascination.

Tragedy for the novice is comedy for the professed. The tragedy of the professed is tragedy for the novice.

Only the sinful are forgiven. Only the sinful forgive others. Only the sinful can forgive themselves.

Those who are imperfect without knowing it mortify us. They are our hope for the next life.

Those who are perfect without knowing it charm us. They are our hope for this life.

Conversion of manners is the wonder-filled life-long transition from the tedium of being other people to the exquisite pleasure of being oneself.

# THE LUCKY *KABUKI*:  FRAGMENTS OF A PLAY

*Personae dramatis:*

Miss *Yoko Kimono* in her hand, fingering, a well-thumbed mass market 800 page abridged edition of THE LIFE OF MISS *YOKO KIMONO,* wearing a butterfly-patterned black *kimono*, rhinestone studded cigarette stick, as herself (né: E.G.A.).

The Proprietor:  in white, three-piece suit, soft white shoes, socks and white panama hat, ruby ring on right hand, diamond wedding band on left, *havana cigarillo*, as himself (né: J.J.A.).

etc.

\*

ACT ONE

*Yoko Kimono*
singing her solo,
*"Alone, O, So, Alone."*

in the new movie,
"The Lucky *Kabuki,"*

as she flicks them into
the ashtray near the
cash register
her cigarette ashes
turn to butterflies
that match her *kimono*.

# CANNA LILY

First
canna lily
comes
virginal,
original, solitary.
Others, of
equal beauty,
come
unnoticed.


# CANNA BLOSSOM

Canna blossom,
bronze and red gold,
on four-foot green scepter,
I call young monk to homage your
beauty,
another plucks
you for his Lady.


# THE MONASTERY:  A SATIRE

In the monastery with soft-ware talk and
in the monastery with harmonic convergence:
white monastery turns wise men
chessnuts and monastic peace
makes monks soldiers.
Bakery with confectioner's
misapprehensions,
monks wreathed in the Bible
heat belt.

Comics and cauldrons of
economic dissonance turn
mellifluous cash registers
and gypsy serenades
beyond all security precautions.

In white monastery with emu
speculations and ostrich
elegance, tractors advance
in olympian ranks like space-age
gladiators.  Haystackers' blues.

The deer know and profess stability,
sixteen in a row, this side of
Highway 212.  Ornithologists' nightmare.

It all comes out
in the imagination.


# DISAPPOINTMENT #2

I am the
reincarnation
of Oscar Wilde.

The good sinner
has become
the
bad monk.

# POEM FOR PAMELA HAMILTON

"Chattanooga, Tenn.—Pamela Hamilton, who became the center of national controversy when her family tried to stop treatment of her bone cancer for religious reasons, died Thursday. She was 14."

*THE ATLANTA CONSTITUTION*
Friday, March 29, 1985

All around you raged a hellish warfare:
scientists
and religionists,
legalists, all
at each other in
your name,
and for those who cared
and those who cried,
some slow consolation.
You proclaimed the
truce with your body.
And your soul
rests in peace——
awaiting Resurrection.


# ENDING

My eyes frame
through aluminum
glass and screen
a year's end scene
of pine wood and
silver sky.


# TARNISHED KNIGHT

Tarnished knight
in breastplate dented,
Desire's thrall inflames

you.  From noble quest
so quickly wrested,
sin's metalled arms
bend to banish
youth's Truth.  Banns
banned in the banishing,
ideals rended like conquered
heraldry, each honeyed strand
of innocence is sundered
by ashy comb.

# THAT HOPE MUST DIE

*"What is your substance, whereof are you made,*
*That millions of strange shadows on you tend?"*

William Shakespeare, *SONNET* 53:1-2


1.  Of him:
after all was said
and done
we would have
only what we
already do
he belongs to you

After burning
and cooling too
he already
belongs to you

2.  Of them:
the same

3.
Sometimes it happens
in that particular
harmony of movements
that hesitant moment
of yes of letting go
or no of trying to contain
to maintain within
to constrain. . .

*"Recalcitrance of the body,"* somebody put it!
*"It doesn't matter to me,"* you once said

4.

An image across the screen
of consciousness
you pass
a form a movement of
light and beauty
silent and serene
or so you seem I know better
but deny your
reality to myself
I need you to
redeem me from
my loneliness
and I know you cannot
you are not
who you seem.

5.

I cannot contain you.  I cannot contain myself.
Half-way to heaven, half-way to hell
we live a dismal existence because we are
torn from above and from below.
Our natures both desire heaven and cause
our own hell.
Your love for me burns hostile in an instant.
You scorch me with your eyes
so blue, so cool, so confused.
Your vulnerability, your very gentility is your
charm
and my destruction.
I cannot contain you nor can you.
If you are a mystery to me
what must you be to yourself?

6.

I loved you from the first tear-stained
glance I caught in a house called God's and
you in conversation with someone else.
Later you said it was of laughter, but
subsequently cried many times in his presence.
I still see your hand reach to catch the tears
or was it a gesture to him in disguise.

Ten years dissolved in your smile,
your crazy close and distancing eyes.
You know yourself so much and so little,
my ambivalent friend.

And I let you play with me—a petty
entertainment
in your boredom, a sincere searching with
someone you hold as one above you
you kill us both.

7.

But I will not let you kill the you in me.
Heavy work with all the rest, rough and coarse
and crude, but you fool only you—your mask
is too plain, the strings are tears on your face.
Your body is a mirror of eternity.  Your
corruption
only a contention in my head with cruelly
demanded
realities.  Your abundant presence in my head,
your
absence in physical form—a shadow of hope, a
glimmer of deeper desired meaning.

8.

I feel you in my thoughts.  I hold you in
aspirations,
red brick homes and colonial columns.
You embrace a child clumsily in your arms.
You pass him to me only in momentary relief.
You reign as prince of the guests of honor at
your own
gathering.
I don't know you.  You know me so well, and so
little.
The more you come into yourself, the less your
fear of
someone so fearsome as me.  You fear yourself.  I
mirror not only your imperfections.  I mirror your
perfections to you, but there is no possibility of
your seeing from the stance you are in.

# STRAIGHTFORWARD SPIRITUAL DESIRES

Mountain bear fur and brown wool
*Juan de la Cruz* white
sailor suits
hiking boots
and Count Chocola cereal
garlic and herbal tea
soda pop and pop star
dancers disco monkey
and straightforward
spiritual desires

Your virtue is kindness
your color blue
*macramé* and yoga
cocky and cocksure
you always speak in
Absolutes sometimes
never generalize maybe

Your impulsiveness gets
you into trouble
but you're loved for your
spontaneity


# LIGHT LIKE ICE, LIGHT LIKE FESTAL RIBBONS

A.M.

the mica sparkles
the sand
the sun illumines the
tin barn roof
ice like glass Christmas ribbons
hangs on the fence
I taste freedom

P.M.

black splotches in the evening
birds perched
on electric lines in twilight
flight
from green-gray day
to night
I taste freedom


## MOON: 5:13 A.M.

Moon—pearl cupped in
a hand of clouds
fisted like a pirate's prize
in this cloistered galleon.


## *KENSHO* (INSIGHT!)

commemorating the day
when the learner
became teacher
the child father
to the man

in the soul
of his brother
in Christ

## *SATORI* (A STATE OF MIND)

II Nocturns 5:00 A.M.

The Void
is the breeze
that fans
the flame
of my
No-Self.
Yes!


## LAUDATION FOR A BROTHER (ON THE OCCASION OF NOTHING IN PARTICULAR HAPPENING) FROM A BROTHER IN CHRIST

Brother:

This monastery
may crumble
into
the sea

But with
you and me
here
the
Noble Effort
will
survive,
the Noble Endeavor
will
Endure!

# THE LIBRARY OGRE

They warned me he could be difficult.
Rules. Order. No nonsense.
Blunt questions. No answers.

They warned me he could be demanding.
Three books, returned at this time.
No more. No later.

They could not have told me how different
it would be. How two brothers
would meet.

I cannot tell you what I mean
if your interpretation is literal.
No blood-line flows, you see.

We met in the presence of another college friend,
before my second daughter,
before my first daughter would be.

He seemed shy and short, stockier than me,
maybe even stodgy, but not stuffy by any means.

Next day, a day of labor it would be,
though studies and silence
were a bit foreign to me.

Silence. Hard research and writing labor.
Then he said: *"Would you like a cup of tea?"*
with a smile as big as a beam,
shining from him to me.

# TO THE MONK WHO WARMS OUR NOT-SO-HOLY SPIRITS

Startle to the tongue,
you're the rum
at the bottom of
the community's mug.

I've never acquired
a taste for such.
For me, a soft red wine,
a little at a time,
with music and books.

These men are rum
drinkers, most, at
least.  And rum will
warm a cold heart
any dark night.

Red wine's fine for clear
evenings, when things
settle, like the clouds
around the sleepy sun.

So let's have more rum,
but in thimbles for the
slow and not so hale
of spirit.

# FOUR POEMS FOR A CHILDREN'S CHRISTMAS PAGEANT

1.

With candlelight and paper lanterns
We prepare His Way the Prince of Peace!

2.

Quickly goes my sleepy yawn
As Angel choirs sing their song!

3.

Lonesome sorrow passes by
As Christmas star greets Winter sky!

4.

My sadness passed with the night
When I met God's Family in Bethlehem!


# PHYSIQUE/OR DIALOGUE OF
# A TEEN-AGER AND HIS MIRROR

take soles
take toes
take calves
and knees and
thighs

take arms
take hair
and navel and
sides

take torso
take pectorals
take shoulders
and throat and veins

take your soles and
take your toes and
take your bones
and calves and
knees and thighs

take your arms and
hair and
navel and sides

take your torso
take your pectorals
and shoulders and
throat and veins

take your knuckles
and biceps


## LOVE AT AGE TWENTY

Gross!
Turn off that song!

I hate slow music!
That's what girls want
you to listen to while
you're with them!

Every song by Hank is great!

Hand me that case of fish
sticks!

I'm doing something
for her no one else
has made me do!

Now I'm listening to shit!

# MOON OVER TEAL STREET

Moon over Teal Street:
water oaks float
through the mist,
rafts of hard wood,
sails of night film over
littered leaves.

Moon over Teal Street:
you are now slowly
fading from our memories.


# RUDDY ROMEO

Ruddy Romeo
decided to slow
down his randy
pace.
After rending
his tormented
soul,
a monk he
became,
and now grows
under
sanctifying
grace.

# THE PIRATE AND HER POET

He turned his lute to
the *timbre* of her voice
and circled her with song,
chording seas of melody
and rhyme.

To sail his
seas of
melody she
did rejoice.

She sang his words and
wrapped him in her charm,
swirling capes across his
brawny arms.

They sailed for shores
north and south,
westerly and east,
with billowed sails
and joy for their feast.

# RESPLENDENT SUN, ARISE!

Resplendent Sun, arise! Up, *Helios,*
out from the murky sea of my
Aegean dreams. Discovered, I salute you,
shimmering, flaring in the sky.
Resplendent Sun, advance! Forward, *Phoebus,*
slay, brass-thoraxed hoplite, my heart's
Pythian woes. Swell my spirit with golden gifts:
joy, music—love's first compatriots.
Resplendent Sun, ascend! High, *Nomios,*
from your *Magna Graecia* confines,
pastor my years. I enshrine you, like *Augustus,*
my vaulted prayers your Palatine.
   In Apollo's sardion forms you course through my life;
   He only was Christ's lamp bearer: You are Christ's eyes!

## LOVE, DREW

When love to love was given,
love drew new love from without,
and forged a compact under heaven:
this man for this maid—no doubt!
When life to life was granted,
life drew new life from inside,
one soul in one flesh fashioned:
and man and wife swelled with pride!
When home from home was built,
home drew new home from within,
framed with care and covered it:
all three nailed tighter than kin!
   Love, Drew, drew you out of mystery:
   life and home now draw your destiny.


## DAPPLED HART

Dappled hart on humus wet,
your keen eye blazes me.  More
action's dart than choices met,
you're ev'ning's unsought reward.
Like dumbed trumpets, brass
bars measure silence's sunset,
and twilight's hues cast
your suede coat all a'russet.
Fleet of foot yet sure of pace,
you pose before serrated pines,
then mock me, cunctative,
and spring the cumulus lines.
   Hart, preserve heart of youth;
   age comes in a moment's truth.

# THE OWL AND THE TIGER

One, fleckèd, looms the woodlands of the brain.
One, chevroned, roams the jungles of the gut.
They're feathered and furrèd, taloned and fanged.
They flare and flail, fighting in endless undefeat.
*"Who?" "Who?" "O—o!" "O—o!"* mocks the aggressor.
*"So repressed and cautious, you sulky fowl!"*
*"You! Chaos! Furor! The stupidity of anger!"*
*"Tender only in the meat!"* fleers the observer.
One roars, so proud in his angularity,
but roars in defense against his own fears.
One, high in learning's tree, hoots haughtily,
but hoots to shoo his doubts and hide away his tears.
 The moon-eyed owl, the tiger of flash action:
 these tawny beasts merge in human integration.


# DARK FRIENDS OF JESUS

Remember so sweet in our childhood, lovely, veiled
Sister pleading: *"Never forget Jesus' words, 'Follow thou Me!'"*
How handsome Father from his black pompomed biretta pulled
holy cards inscribed in gold filigree: *"Always an 'Alter Christus' be!"*
But those girlish ears and boyish eyes were doubly deaf and blind:
in glorious innocence, and ignorance of the impending years;
of how becoming "another Christ" takes more than being kind,
takes terror and torment and courage through the tears.
Sister knew, Father knew, and we, each in the silence of our hearts:
silver wings and rubied crowns befit a child's faith;
One only is the Lord, soaked in blood, his hat a cap of thorns,
and we need do nothing 'cept say *"Yes"* when he calls us to be his friends.
 Whatever our past, whatever our present, whatever be our pain.
 We are all dark friends of Jesus, each known to Him by name.

## SOMETIMES

Sadness sometimes swells your mind,
though you dare not let it known:
sadness you feel makes you slight,
and to the world must seem strong.
Loving sometimes swells your heart,
though you'd never speak the word:
loving's just passing regard,
deft thrusts of a human sword.
Self-loss sometimes swells your soul,
and you fear you'll not endure:
self-loss, loss of all control,
to rule your life your grandeur.
  Sometimes these vicissitudes:
  But forever you'll be you!


## TIMELESS YOUTH

Ardent Adonis, I fear to ask
how fares last week's sweet:
six days only now have passed,
might I a new Venus meet!
Agile Apollo, please recall,
Virgin Daphne, fleeing you,
transformed into shapely laurel
tree, to foil your match untrue
Ruddy Romeo, do not forget,
eyes still wet in pining,
you, in wooing darling Juliet,
broke vows with dear Rosaline!
  Timeless youth, eternal dissembler:
  you haste to waste your treasure!

# SOMEDAY

As you feel now, someday I'll feel strong,
and shoulder to shoulder we'll bear arms.
Like Achilles and Patroclus at Troy,
I'll kill any Hector who dares you harm.
As you look now, someday I'll look great,
and arm against arm we'll strut the streets.
Veronan Valentine and Proteus,
I'll to you fair Silvia bequeath.
As you are now, someday I'll be good,
and head to heart we will fill our years,
Evangelist John and scribe Prochorus,
whispering across lonely Aegean.
    I pin your corduroy cap to my wall;
      for now:  heel, regret, age, truth above all.


# SENSES OF A FRIEND

1.
Intermittent as silence
pulsing music from noise:
you purpose speech.

2.
Recurrent as blink of light
in night's storm:
you steer sight.

3.
Alternate as fasting
cleansing the tongue:
you purify taste.

4.
Absent as emptiness
shaping matter to form:
you guide touch.

5.
Periodic as breeze
in a fragrant garden:
you perfume breathing.

6.
Sensible as black sky
beneath fireworks' burst:
you give constancy to ecstasy.

7.
Sensitive son to God,
lover, father and friend:
you are nobility within humanity.


## MY SHADOW'S FRIEND

Pool of cool peace beneath lava's blast;
Rose fragrant grown from thorny stem;
Snoozle cat house-bound in lion's wrath;
Brusque Boaz, Ruth asleep your hem.
Pearl-diving seas of unconscious mind;
Speaking easily with *devas;*
trading pulses with animal kind;
Climbing peaks of arcane scriptures.
*"Owe no debt to another except*
*it be that of love,"* scripted Christ-
consumed Saul.  Goodness' ledger,
gifts, coins can't cancel, words least.
   Our gentle Jesus in Baptist's skins;
   indebt me more, my shadow's friend!

## AGAIN

Quick, calm, and confident,
controlling course of my blood;
Quiet, in clear cadences,
guiding flow of my moods.
Guaranteeing new hopes
with mind-powders, heart-agents,
you twine, draw chemical ropes
to uncurtain dark stages.
Judgeless, evocative,
listening kind as a priest,
you invite me on to live
from sorrows more released.
   I, one of thousands viewed:
   Again, Jesus heals through you.


## FOREVER UPON A RAINBOW

Once upon a memory, twice upon a tune,
You hoped someday you'd help somebody,
Now we come to you in throngs,
Thrice upon a thought, four upon a melody.
Five times upon a daydream you listen for your name;
Your little ones say, *Momma,* Old folks, *Mam,*
Only your spouse, *Sweetheart,* most of us, *Charlene,*
Six times upon a minute, seven when we can.
You have eight or nine hundred different faces,
For at least ten thousand more it seems,
Speak warm consoling words in cold tiny laces,
Beam brilliant smiles over office telephones.
   In desiring to heal the Universe, you're absolutely best;
   And forever upon a rainbow you'll serenely glide to rest.

# THE GENTLE DECEPTION

In the seminary
I drank Twining tea
and read H. D. Thoreau.
The Trappists have
taught me how to enjoy
dark beer, the Superbowl
and women.
I wanted to be a hermit
back then,
like my hero—T. Merton.
Now I know he wasn't
and I can't be so.
My brothers in Christ
are calling me to
run, not crawl,
give, not cry,
live, not die.
Trappist peace
is inside me like an unfinished poem.


# A LITTLE POEM FOR A GLORIOUS PERSON

Hannah!

Glorious things take
—God's own time—
an eternity to make.

Now we have you with us.

And thus we'll all continue
for eternity in our loving
—in God's own time.

## THE GENTLE GIANT

With one punch
you could knock me
dead, yet
you pat me
on the back.

With one stomp
you could break my
feet,
instead
you invite me
to walk ahead.

With a glare
you could hurt me
hard,
but you warm my
heart
with your smile.

You're a lot like Jesus,
and too good to
ever dare
think that
of yourself.


## THE *CLOISONNÉ* CUP

Melancholy veins
through your
being
like gold wire
in a *cloisonné* cup,
a lament for your
boyhood lost,
a search for
the unloved son.

You desire the
young, and the
bright and the
beautiful, and
Our Lord comes
in the intervening
years, in the
dark and the
wounded, to be
healed through you,
to heal you through
them, because you
are young and bright
and beautiful, in His
heart, in His Spirit.


## ALESSANDRA: A SONNET

In thy eyes, undefined, green, blue, brown, gold,
vision for mine eyes, blinded, I hope.
In thy fingers, tiny, pink, pearl, rose, gold,
extension of mine own reach, too defined, I hope.
In thy mind, receptive, magnetic, pure, still,
pulse for mine own life, unloving, I seek.
In thy soul, expansive, with wonderment all-filled,
enlargement for mine own soul, constrained, I pray.
In thy full-being, exquisite, with light all-filled,
sole victory, marginal enough, over gloom, I pray.
   Alessandra, thy name befits thy beauty.
   In thee,  our God recapitulates Divinity.

# PEREGRINATIO ALESSANDRAE

**1.**

In ancient days, when *Episcopoi* walked
the roads of Rome, vested in senatorial
splendour, when pagans and believers talked
in antique tongue, Eastward journeyed Egeria.

**2.**

In these the days of our own passing, as august
abbot, mitred, priest, malachite robed, brother,
cowled, as cenobites search for Christ in the south,
Northward, to be received, journeyed Alessandra.

**3.**

She came in magnificence attired, a great
diadem of sunbeams upon her head,
sapphire orbs of water flowing through her eyes,
her arms zircon scepters silencing speech.

**4.**

Mystic progenitors kneeling along her way,
slow-bowing bicorn, musical, of white velour,
dumb-struck sinners, guilt-ridden, blushing in shame,
all made obeisance to her irenic nature.

**5.**

In ancient days, when *Presbyteroi* healed
souls in the East, Westward went Egeria.
In these our days of newly inspired feelings,
we could but weep when homeward went Alessandra.

# THIS NIGHT

This night
the moon
is the death mask
of Keats
and clouds pass
as repeated
quatrains
in a
starry sonnet.

## "FEELS JUST LIKE THE HANK WILLIAMS, JR., BLUES AGAIN"

1. Proud of my Bandit all blue and shiny chrome.
   Proud of those 1/2 million candles on its dome.
   It's what Hank drives. Why not me?

2. Carry me liquor tucked in belt.
   Rattlesnake band on my hat of black felt.
   Think Hank looks tough? Don't mess with me!

3. Wear my jeans tight and wear my boots tall.
   Wear white on dates most of all.
   Think Hank dazzles? Girls, take a look at me!

4. Not ashamed to call people what they are.
   Not ashamed for tryin' to set the world on fire.
   Hank's the greatest thing goin' after me!

5. Give a damn about people wherever I go.
   Please don't ask me to tell them so.
   Hank's not "sensitive." Certainly not me!

6. Now even monks come for spiritual chats.
   Don't have time for things like that.
   Hank's got the answers. Question him, not me!

7. Can't handle all this stuff called "LIFE."
   Hard workin'. Not sleepin'. Women who want to be my wife.
   Must be how Hank feels? He's a lot like me!

8. Goin' on twenty-one and feel almost forty-two.
   Agin' fast from all of you.
   Oh, Hank, please pull me through!

## "AIN'T THIS BOB DYLAN'S BLUES AGAIN?"

1. Loopin' across the Parkway off Exit 78.
   Spinnin' my wheels through the gate.
   Playin' a game of chance with time and fate.
   Ain't this Bob Dylan's blues again?

2. Turn off the radio and turn on the smile.
   March through the door like a soldier on file.
   Or crawl like a criminal on his way to trial.
   Ain't this Bob Dylan's blues again?

3. Cast glances at those cashier girls.
   Nod to bruisers openin' cans with their nails.
   Dodge rowdies swingin' from the ceiling rails.
   Ain't this Bob Dylan's blues again?

4. Try to think up somethin' that's cute.
   Throw words around like bullets that shoot.
   Ask questions like pirates diggin' for loot.
   Ain't this Bob Dylan's blues again?

5. Turn conversations into duels of illusion.
   Scramble the sequence to add some confusion.
   Falsely apologize for calculated intrusions.
   Ain't this Bob Dylan's blues again?

6. Make a pretense of fun by bein' serious.
   Hide the emptiness by bein' mysterious.
   Joke with ease while feelin' furious.
   Ain't this Bob Dylan's blues again?

7. Pull skulls from imaginary top hats.
   Watch cadavers rise from freezer vats.
   See phantoms swirl over electric mats.
   Ain't this Bob Dylan's blues again?

8. Hear pained infants weep like the night's rain.
   Pass out vest pocket poems from a curious brain.
   Slip away fast like the next movin' train.
   Ain't this Bob Dylan's blues again?

9. Circlin' back home at a dangerous rate.
   Wonderin' whether I'm feelin' small or great.
   Knowin' all along I'm Delusion's mate.
   Ain't this Bob Dylan's blues again?

10. A cloud of dust settles over my head.
    Part of me's alive and part of me's dead.
    An angel sleeps with a demon in my bed.
    Ain't this Bob Dylan's blues again?

## "THEN, *'YES!'*, MY LOVE"

Remember your hearing so long ago,
Our Master's voice in soft tones,
Inviting you to Him follow,
And forge heartward a homeless home.
Remember your saying again and again:
*"Oh, Master, I'm afraid and unsure.*
*My weakness I know and fear my pain.*
*Do you, please, help me perdure."*
*"Take care to love yourself always.*
*Take love from My care in time.*
*Take peace from pain all your days.*
*Take peace from all hearts in life."*
    Then, *"Yes!, My Love,"* I say today;
    And know, always, you are my way.


## OH, JESUS!

To open your heart is a fearful task,
yet the mandate
of Our Lord.

To break your heart
is a fearsome take,
yet the gift given
from Our Lord.

Your heart will be
shattered,
and your heart
will be healed
as you yourself
choose.

To lie about yourself
is more painful
than to cry.

And to die is the
least painful
call for us all
when our time
is His time.


## BITE OF YOUTH

Your softness amazes me,
fluttering dove on my wrist,
more fluff than anatomy,
captured in a finger's twist.
Augh!  Snap-jawed fangs needle stitch
through flesh taut with straining.
Get gone!  Get free!  No way!  Which
smarts more:  wound or the wounding?
Nefarious viper?  No!
Only verbal bite of youth,
one most curious to know,
to exact, truth told for told truth.
    Gentle lad, yet dangerous
    in wisdom, I respect you!


## "I CAN HANDLE IT!"

I can handle work:
I'm young!
I can handle her:
she's my wife!
I can handle her:
she's my daughter!
I can handle him:
he's my son!

Can I handle work?
(when I'm strong)
Can I handle my wife?
(when she loves me)

273

Can I handle my daughter?
(when she kisses me)

Can I handle my son?
(when he touches me)

Lord Jesus, I can handle it!
(when everyone and you help me).


## PROVIDENCE

The egg must be cracked
before you can bake.
The dough must be kneaded
before you get cake.
The apple must be sliced
before you get sauce.
We all must be weakened
before we get strong.


## THE SERPENT AND THE DOVE

MATTHEW 10:16

They thought, perhaps, they'd
nestle you, a dove, in their
hand, and they did, as
long as they could understand.

They thought, perhaps, they'd
tame you, a dove, in their
hand, but you bit, a serpent
by surprise:  Freedom,
never in the hand.

They tried to compress you
in their fist, and you bit
them:  free-spirited, you will not
be constrained.


## THE CONQUEST OF DEFEAT

The conquest of defeat:
last public articulation
of an old self-image.

The conquest of defeat:
what a lesson from
a young man who professed no belief
in the Resurrected Christ.


## THE WINE PRESS

Like fine wine
I'm getting better
with age:
being in
the wine press
for the last
four years
has helped me
appreciate peace.


## THE WOODBURNING STOVE

One log for my husband, just us two.
Two logs for the pretty one who made us three.
Three logs for our baby in all her fears.
Four logs for my family wherever they be.
Five logs for my friends, helpful in need.
Six logs for us all, burning in the stove.

Seven logs, with my love, Lord, firing my heart.
Splinters of hope charged to flares in the dark.
Warm my coldness, Lord, I feel so alone.
Blaze me in my blackness.  Make this heart your home.
Teach me trust, Lord.  This pain won't do me harm.


## THE SHEDDING OF ILLUSIONS

One log for my youth's love, just us two.
Two logs for my daughter, she made three.
Three logs for my small one and her fear.
Four logs for my family wherever they be.
Five logs for kind friends close in need.
Six logs for our world burn in the stove.
Seven logs, with yours, Lord, all aflame.
Splinters of hope all aflame in the dark.
Warm my coldness, Lord.  Melt these tears.
Teach me trust, Lord.  Keep away all harm.
Show this night's but deep sleep of dawn.
Turn my heart's emptiness to sought home.
I'm just a fragile child asleep in Your arms.

## AWARENESS

"It's a table"

"No, it's not a table.  It's a building."

"No, it's not a building. It's a man."

"No, it's not a man.  It's a church."

"No, it's not a church.  It's a lady."

"No, it's not a lady.  It's a people."

"Well, then it's a man!"

"Yah, and a woman!"

"No, not just a man.  It's an old guy.  He
died back when."

"Yah, but this is a lady too."

"Well, she died.  She's older than he is.
And, besides, some say she didn't die."

"What a guy!  What a lady!"

"She's not a lady.  She's a man."

"She looks like a lady to me!"

"Well, what you see is not what you get!"

"Well, I don't get it. Table, Building. Man. Lady, Old.
Dead. Not dead. Anyway, she looks like a man to me."
"What's goin' on here?  All these people standing in a line?
All these people making food and giving it away.  Looks like a table to me."

*

"Let's get something straight. The 'solution' department's down there. This is the 'doing' department."
"We've got clothes. Keep your spandex and glitter-glasses for Halloween. Here's the real stuff: cotton, polyester, some wool, once in a while a little cashmere, even a piece of gold *lamé.*"

\*

"What's going on here? I thought that guy in the middle ages was poor."
"And besides, why don't these people work? And why are they always coming back?"

\*

"Well, because this is a table."

"And you get food at a table."

"And this is a building."

"And this is quite a dude. Saint Francis. He cared."

"And besides, the lady who died or didn't die is Mary, God's Mother."

"She wore gold *lamé* when God made her."

"All these guys and all these ladies are brothers and sisters."

"She's our Mother."

"And she's a church because she's a people who care. "

"She's priests. She's babies."

"She's cooks and eaters. Hatters and wearers."

"She's ill but she's strong."

"She hurts but she's loving."

"Sometimes she wants to give up."

\*

"She's a he and he's an us and we're SAINT FRANCIS TABLE at the SHRINE!"

# SHRINE OF THE IMMACULATE CONCEPTION

There is
a gracious
Victorian Lady
who
has built
her mansion
of wood and brick
and stone
and sleeps
all alone
in elegance
among the rubble.
She is an
ancient idea
encased
in woman.


## "...QUAM ADMIRABILE EST..."

"...*quam admirabile est...*"
you heave your chest
in careful Latin diction.

"...*quam admirabile est...*"
thus foreign-tongued—
your inner sentiments best
expressed—in antique meter.

"...*quam admirable est...*"
a form for ballet, a mind
for debate, the *proscenium*
your natural setting.

"...*quam admirable est...*"

# SIR CONLEY AND MEDINA

Lunges of your lance
the crest of your *bassinet*
the boss of your shield.

Pommel and *cantels* of
your battle saddle
slip in instability.

The dubbing and the *collé*
long forgotten. *"Which commandment did
you break:*

1. false judgement or treason, *pite?*
2. honor with women, *courtoisie?*
3. Mass each day?"

Your cracked *greaves* lie beside
your shattered *eventail*, no more
masks, no more strutting and stirrups.
Medina, Sir Conley, has stolen
your innocence.


# ANGEL OF LIGHT

A configuration of
light
beamed down from
heaven
to delight
and
enlighten us.

# ORDER OF JUSTICE/ORDER OF MERCY

Look to Christ and ask: *"What is our relationship?"*
*"What do you want of me?"*

Infinity of compassion...
Look to yourself:
more unforgiving than all of these...
Look to your wife:
boundless as a human heart can be...
Look to your children:
they want you out of their need...
Look to your work:
there is a care mitigated by greed...
Look to your relatives:
they must be set free...
Look to your friends:
you must simply let them be.

\*


Can I say: *"Yes"* to Christ?
Can I say: *"Yes"* to myself?
My wife?
My children?
My work?
My relatives?
My friends?
If my answer is *"No,"* what must I do?
What must I change?

# WHY DID YOU COME TO THE MONASTERY?

Why did you come to the monastery?

To become a Saint.

Wonderful!  How are you going to do that?

By being a good monk.

Wonderful!  How are you going to do that?

By being faithful to our tradition.

Wonderful!  How are you going to do that?

By keeping our vows.

Wonderful!  How are you going to do that?

By being faithful every day.

Wonderful!  How are you going to do that?

By doing what I should do.

Wonderful!  How are *YOU* going to do that!!


# I'LL NEVER CLAIM YOUR CHIN

I'll never claim your chin
was carved by Canova,
hardly!

Nor that blush the
brush strokes of Botticelli,
surely!

Nor those fingers wings over the entrance of Vezaley,
really!

Yet I'll go into the
Georgia clay believing
you're a God-send,
truly!


## ANGEL OF PRAYER

Angel of prayer to
encourage me
in darkest mood.

Messenger of fire to
purify me.

Burn into brass
heat.


## *GINKGO* TREE

*Ginkgo* tree,
half
frost-eaten
warmed
by
the concrete,
we
revere
you.

# A BORROWED INHERITANCE

Fleshly swords from fleshly
conquests contract.  And love
not born from love like scorched
rose withers.  Swords of spirit
to spirit's quest thrust.  And
love great born from love like
leaves from sheaths stretch.
Sorrow's sword cracked by joy's
sword shatters.  Blade to blade
clang strange against youth's
moods and man's lordly manners.
Plumed passion and pommelled
peace:  each war within us.
Thus, youth, countenance the man
within.  And win!

# MARKET NOTES

## GLOSSARY

Magrophobia:   the feeling I had during my first stop at Market Grocery

BMW:   before meeting William; or: same as above

ALG:   aging Love Generation

BMAY:   before meeting all of you; see Margrophobia above; see BMW above

MLC:   mid-life crisis; see ALG above

NP:   not-perverted; or; the realization that I'm a member of ALG (see above); or; I'm experiencing MLC just like other guys my age (see above); or; being "normal" complicated by being socially abnormal; see Monk below

MONK:   see "socially abnormal," NP part three above

Margrophilia:   the feeling I have for Market Grocery

THANKS:   SEE ALL OF THE ABOVE

\*

## "SEEMS I'VE GOT THE BOB DYLAN BLUES ONCE AGAIN"

For the Brothers in the Meat Department

1. I play air guitar better than anyone in sight.
   Mimic harmonica notes with all my might.
   Yeh, Bob! How about me?

2. I'm almost forty-two and act like I'm twenty-one.
   I'm supposed to be serious and want to have fun.
   Oh, Bob! What's happenin' to me?

3. I've got spiritual insights and wisdom beyond my years.
   Wish I could wear a top hat around my ears.
   Great Bob! Why you, not me?

4. Oh God! I go to youngsters to make me feel good.
   Someday I'll wear my robes and wear my hood.
   Whoever Bob is, I've got to be me.

\*

DIALOGUE

| | |
|---|---|
| Nancy: | "What are you doing here today?" |
| John: | "I came to see William for spiritual direction." |
| Nancy: | "WILLIAM!?!" |
| Aubrey: | "Hello, John!" |
| Robert: | "Hey, John!" |
| Jimmy about Caitlin: | "The little lady is doin' fine!" |
| Dave about John: | "Michael, there goes your recommendation." |
| Michael: | "Doesn't it make you SAD that you'll never have children? |
| John to himself: | "How do I answer this? If I say 'No' he'll think something is wrong with me. If I say 'Yes' he'll think I'm unhappy and that's not really true either." |
| John to Michael: | "To quote William's favorite word: *'Sometimes.'*" |
| John to Jeff Hall: | "My writings are my children. People don't take me seriously when I say that." |
| Jeff: | "I do. The people here are your spiritual children too." |
| William: | "I'm much too macho to wear an earring!" |

287

| | |
|---|---|
| Derron to John at first meeting: | "How do you feel about priests who don't keep their promises?" |
| Michael to Derron: | "That's too personal to ask." |
| Sean to John at first meeting: | "Why did you become a monk?" |
| John to himself: | "To tell the truth that I felt called by Christ seems too simple. . .more complex than that. How do I explain my whole life to someone I don't know?" |
| John to Sean: | "Two women committed suicide when I told them I would not marry them. I entered the monastery to do penance." |
| Nancy to John: | "I'll say hello for you when I call down to Panama City." |
| Steve: | "McBye! [or is that 'Mac-buy!'?]" |

\*

The ambivalence of values. The intention of communication. Disturbed silence. Living in the isolation of misplaced needs. Is it neediness?

\*

Work. Working through the emotions. Learning the difficulties of first and second and third love. Street wise is more than woman wise. Book wise is more than school wise. Who knows more? Who's the stronger for it all?

\*

Last times are first times. Last time was the last time, not the next time.

\*

*

We learn lessons of victory by defeat.
We learn our wantedness by rejection.
We learn peace by warfare.
We learn need by dejection.
You learn but don't listen.
You hope but you don't strive.
You strive against all hope.
I hear and learn.
I learn from hearing.
I strive and do not win.
I win by striving.

*

Bad timing leads to bad days.
Bad days flow from bad timing.
Listening to needs is work.
Not working leads to bad timing.
Bad learning leads to new listening.
New listening. New listening.

Staying away is a desired presence.
Presence leaves much to be desired.
The uncertainty of choice. Not valid!
Leading against productive efforts.
Energy displaced.

Eventually there comes a time when the decision reached
through insight must be acted upon. We cannot have it
all ways.

Change does not come from intellectual clarity. Intellectual
clarity is the result of change in thinking. But behavioral
change comes from change in behavior.

To act foolishly is to act out of harmony with one's true
state in life. It is an act without prudence. It is
to act without awareness. It is to act without
circumspection.

Wisdom is gained at the cost of one's reputation.

Knowledge is accumulated information, not wisdom.

To be wise is to act in accord with one's nature; it is
to follow the course of truth as disclosed in time.
Wisdom is openness to the revelation of reality
within and all around us.

*

The inevitable redistribution of forces,
the energies displaced, the recharging
of impulses, the recreation of images,
projections from the past, projections
into the future.

Each one a separate entity, a model
of emotional enclosure, a vulnerability
which shields itself against the onslaught
of unpleasant sensations.

The horizontal moods, the pain unarticulated
to self, let alone to others.
Fend off the pain. It wears youth's face.

The time traversed. Two years of successful
redistribution of self-wrought images.

All these latinizations for loss and gain.
To have come, to have met, to move on.
Where? Into deeper self.

*

## THE CLOISTER AND THE MARKET PLACE

The country Strat twangs a rhythm,
some sense of cadence in a chaos of
cares, loves, moves, family pain, stretching
youth, arching hopes and sloping dreams.

The historical Jesus is dead and gone, mercilessly
hacked, sundered soul from bone-counted body.
The resurrected Christ buys ground beef dressed in jeans, a
handkerchief tied over her corn-braids.

The country singer croons a rhyme,
some sense of sensibility in a sea of
memories, long-forgotten roads to a home-centered
life, loves broken, cares cast like shattered glass
across the wet floor.  The resurrected Christ
beams a line of warmth through the cold room.
What can be said has been said.  The six
strings have been tuned.  The song is being sung.

A distant plain chant in a grove of magnolia trees
tells the rhythm of the centuries.  The psalms
count out three cycles of hope and despair.  The
country boy buries his heart in a cowl of rough wool.

\*

## "I REMEMBER ME"

He dances in blue jeans
and alligator boots
prances like a matador
before his own bullishness
a pretense

His beltplate's like a
suit of burnished armor
halfway down his
defensiveness

His lance is his laugh
his shield his eyes

Everything in reverse
full-speed in retrospection

Ah, yes!  I was him once:
I remember me in a way I never was.




```
    *
  * * *
    *
    *
    *
```

## OXFORD *SATORI*

Two girls were walking.
Two boys were playing
basketball.
People came and went.
Doors were being locked.
The clock chimed in
quarters.
The stone grave-markers
slept
while Autumn tucked
herself to bed.
I took this leaf
from near the
bench where your
defenses broke down
. . .from that hallowed ground.


## TWO BARS OF BRASS

Two bars of
brass clang
hard when
they clash
in the solitude of life.

# A LETTER TO NOVICE TIMOTHY

Novice Timothy:

Recluse spiders crawl on desks of oak and walnut cut from wood of smiths/you define logic as sets of canasta cards stacked against the ocean front of pine needles cones and surfers of the moon/dialogical oppositions from academicians unknowing of the UNKNOWABLE which is extremely defined, refined, confined to silence and solitude/Waterfront counterfeit mystics signal distances from sleeves of robes made out of animosities of feeling/One often wonders if wonder is remembered at all? In the heat of the evening ice cream melted down the hands of monks welcoming friendly official from Rome white ice cream on monastic beards. Nothing got in the way of the popcorn though and laughter was heard from folks never known to be so self-consciously free of themselves. You get what you take and you make a life out of it. Are you living?

Junior


# TO THE EDITORS OF THE MERTON ANNUAL

Yes, to your lives!
Yes, to your talents!
Yes, to your goodness!
Yes, to your hard work!
Yes, to your unique perspectives!
Yes, to your unique gifts!
Yes, to receiving your critique
of my hard work!
Yes, to all the good things
we've shared over the years!
Yes, to prayer and reflection!

## WE'RE RIGHT ON THE EDGE

We're right on the edge of this thing and nobody's watchin' it but me. . .a new sense of bein' cut off from others and how we once were known. . .of how we're fittin' in with those around us. . .of how to "rebuild" our infrastructures. . .and how to restructure the thing to begin with. . .and, like everybody, we need money. . .and we're on the edge of this thing which is about to happen, which can happen, if we make it happen, and nobody's watchin' it but me.


## POEM FROM COVE CAY

The wicker and the rattan
the sleek blinds slide
like tears of loving and parting
The embrace of hello
and the embrace
of good-bye
and blessings.


## SOME THOUGHTS DURING A COMMUNITY MEETING

I love you, my Lord, my
strength, my Rock, my
Fortress, my Savior, my
God in whom I trust.

I give you thanks for all
the love you give me
through the people who
love you. You touch me
with the tenderness of your
care. Teach me to show
your love in return.

I accept the love you
send. Help me to give
love in return.

I sorrow for the sadness
of the one missing
the loved one gone.  I
rejoice in the gift of
life you give to all
of us, through each
other—all loved
and loving in you.
Amen.


## "EVENING VERSE FOR FOUR"

The moon sparkles gray tonight.  (Brother Love)
New York escapades of light
and laughter. . .(Uncle Joe Hanes)
*"Life is a bowl of cheeries!"*  (Brother Beel)
And the goose swallowed
the pop top.  (Sister Desire)
&
Veronica, by happy coincidence.


## "THIS IS THE WAY I REMEMBER YOU"

Your hair was
the color of
the Dahlia
I gave you.
And glorious
was your
enthusiasm.

You seemed taller
then and I
felt small.  I
see you now,
powerful.  Are
you still you?

## PICASSO SHIMMIES

Picasso shimmies
ball cap on her head
down the pine cone path

dances under the magnolia
branch, to the balance of
a boom-box

Picasso blinks
in sweaters
from a pink skin face

smiles like a CD
whirling in the sun
silver and red-headed

chrome guitar hums
as Picasso pours tea
half-way there is forever


## *"THE HUMOR IN OUR LIFE IS ALWAYS SERIOUS"*

Starched and stiff
Trappist novices we sat
as you, in wooly turtle-neck,

bonged off-the-wall images
of great Saint Jehosophat,
and without a break, levelled
recondite judgements
on monastic things this and that:
*"The humor in our life is always serious!"*

Stunned we were and stuffed
into a medieval moment—you,
above these white-robed *gargoyles,*
declaring ignorance with a *hauberk*

and a *tréfoil:* *"To maintain a distinction*
*between Christianity and other traditions*
*is to still dwell in the realm of*
*metaphysical duality!"*

In an instant up came griffins
prancing across heroic tapestries,
viola-players, stone patriarchs
and prophets from *Rheims* to *St. Michel,*
arabesques and buddhist chanters,
*swamis* humming the *Vedas,*

citations from Theodore of Mopsuestia,
scholastic masters and masters of
the *sacra pagina,* poets and prelates
and *Canticum Canticorum* commentators
from Alexandria to Swineshead.
And with you and them went
our willing wits. *"The seriousness*
*in novices is always funny!"*


## THE FIREFLY SWIMS

The firefly swims in
the nectar of the gladiola.
The lily trumpets to
the lamppost.
The deer graze by the barn.

# A LETTER TO HOLY SNOWFLAKE

Dear Holy Snowflake:

Hope the heat is burning your residual anger, making you light like a goose quill in June, supple like the wind and effervescent. Reports declare that the troops are secure behind observances and sincere accolades for leadership and acquisitions of honor above all else. Defeat is such a sure way to perfection. Pectoral crosses mask human hurts. Taffeta tears smear begonia blossoms on the wayside of fear. Sentries report allowances for humanity. This is a guarantee of something. Racial tension holds the bowstring taut. Use that feather to puncture illusions. You are not the Savior of Mississippi! That job's already been taken care of by another marksman. Matthew, Luke and the Johannine School rewrote the story. Your job is to die in the pure breath of joy. Are you breathing? The monastic table top mosaics brought a moment of sorrow for their seriousness but the pleasure in seeing them was mine truly. Their use will be established by the Death Squad stationed at the paper cutter. You get the point, I'm sure. St. John's Steeple is also known to be a Borgia Beehive. Be careful. You may get stung by the ecclesiasticalism of the verse. Please do not be frightened; it was my dissolution, not yours. Bonsai Masters tickled the troops with hacksaws and sliding boards. The only thing broken was feelings. Everything else stacked up pretty good, considering the helpers they sent us were all blind to start with and only saw the light at midnight. Grace is a descending balloon, coming to your hometown soon. Hope that goose quill doesn't bust it.

Yours in the wisdom of the instant,

*René St. Croix*

P.S. A love poem for a girlfriend 1972, just published.

# THE PRIZED PLUME

1.

Happy dapper feather things
nuzzle into the clay
as tractor grounds out morning calls
to me. I touch the wind with my ears.
The prized plume floats away
and I let it glide.

2.

How many canons of medieval Paris could
write *exempla* with these quills or
New Guinea medicine men heal children?
How many hats in Prague could
wield these speckled plumes or
Anglo-Saxon archers shoot?

3.

How many memories could
you write if I gave you
one duck feather, two goose quills?
What of the wings of mockingbirds
or a hundred peacock tails?
Would that be enough to get you started?

4.

How many hopes I have for
your health as this white
fluff is blown over roots and
pine needles! How many wishes
for another visit as this dapper
beaked thing squacks to me!

5.
How many friends will claim you?

# THE VIEW FROM EXIT 41

This world moves through my mind
like a stream of automobiles
size     color     speed

like an orb of phosphorescence
lasers and electronics and sound

Reality swirls in my heart
like a flow of emotions
short     long     uncertain

My life passes away from me
like the eastbound horizon
almost near     far     gone

I feel no need to name these things
I call them what they are
world     reality     life

Like the murmur of the steady traffic
my consciousness pushes out
to recognized and to newly tracked places

The hearse of my past rolls along this long road

An ambulance delivers me alive
unnamed and untouched by all that is familiar

# THE HUMANITY OF CHRIST

*Fuego, Cruz y Amor:*
a trinity of symbols that spit
and sparkle in the dusk of
this day, a triad of purposes
in the solitude of life.

*Fuego, Cruz y Amor:*
a three-pronged theme of wrought
iron, wood and flame, a pyramid
of logs and heat and light
that split and hiss and flicker.

*Fuego, Cruz y Amor:*
one monk and another monk
and Christ in the Eucharist,
bound by heat and heart
and pain, a community of
healing, hope and happiness.

\*


Three flames dance before me,
tease and tousle in semi-silence,
reminders of passion and pride
and place. Three flames prance
before me like the world, the
flesh and the devil, all in
holy warfare with holy fire,
holy suffering and sacred love.

\*


*Fuego, Cruz y Amor.*

# IN THEIR PRIVATE GRIEFS

I feel the lament
in my soul
as All Saints
tower bells
ring.

The changing oaks
and burnt pine needles
speak of ages past
and people long gone.

The silence from
the bell tower speaks
of vibrant monks and
resounding hearts in
youth, autumn and
the winter of life.

Monks, saints singing
in their private griefs.
Sinners, chanting
in their public praise
as All Hallows Eve
bends over the globe
of nighttime into
reconciliation.

# KEATS

Bands of plumed knights,
and gossamer draped maidens,
wrights and boding spirits.

The masking of reality and
the unveiling of illusion.

*"All Hallow's Eve!"* Whom
better to remember
than John Keats.

# POEM-FAX TO THE PRESIDENT OF THE LAW COMMISSION

Dear Reverend Father:

My thoughts and prayers are with you as you work in the land of the great sonnetwrights. May the spirit of Keats and Shakespeare infuse your canonical concerns with new-found inspiration. And may the sad sage of Oscar, no mean sonneteer in his own right, add pathos and compassion to your deliberations. For my part, I have experienced intense exasperations with regard to the usual melodrama of my quite quiet and ordinary life of voluntary captivity here at Conyers. I've racked the coals into ash at the South River Hermitage and saluted more than one wondrously blazing flash of deer's tail. The hunters are benevolent to this solitary hiker. POEMS progresses toward press-time but without haste. Patrology III: The Eastern Fathers of the Church, begins Monday, November 16. I pity the juniors; this most dull of studies in any formation program is a requirement for them. Only those who have no students can truly teach. Only the student can be a teacher of others. I find myself, by some strange fate, both. I pray the blue jacket wins warmth and comments for your high fashion. I ponder the strange fact that my luggage and clothes have seen parts of the world I never will, in this mortal existence. While I do not consider myself a burden I consider the press of lived reality a constricting dilemma. I am not good enough, lacking courage and real hope, to say with Saint John of the Cross: *"I die because I do not die."* To the contrary, I find that anger invigorates me, balances my chemistry, puts fine blush on my ashen face, and causes me to stand a centimeter taller. Your great furry charioteer declared you were, *"glad to get away."* Who could blame you? Sad returns with such sweet asceticism await November 18th. Before dread Death's countenance my agonies are a piffle. How kind of time my first fax to England is to you, my abbot.

The author of SAINT JOHN'S STEEPLE

305

## ¿YO SOY DURO?

*"El Diós que viven en mi amigo me intiende."*

Hno. Pablo Maria Diez, OCSO

*

*Yoy so duro.*

*Yo soy duro, pero con amor de niño.*
*¡No! ¿Si? ¡Si!*
*Yo soy duro.*

*La vida me he enseñado*
*defenderme asi.*
*¿Pero, como yo soy duro*
*con amor de niño?*
*Porque yo no guardo*
*resentimiento en mi corazon.*

*Yo no creo; pero mi*
*amigo me dijo eso es verdad.*
*¿Como?  ¿Porque me dijo eso?*


He tells me that people do
not understand my intentions,
but see only my actions, hear
only my words.  My friend tells
me he knows of my deep frustrations
for being treated this way for
so many years.

*Yo soy duro por que tengo*
*el espiritu de Tomàs Merton.*
*Pero yo no vivo en el*
*camino de el.  Tengo el*
*espiritu de Tomàs Merton,*
*pero yo tengo mi propio*
*camino.*

*¿Quien me entiende? ¡Diós!*
*¡Solamente Diós! Por eso*
*yo soy duro. Porque solo*
*Diós me entiende.*

And so I find myself in great
darkness when no
human being understands
me. And what is this great
darkness?

*Simplemente, es mi cruz. ¡Ahora, yo*
*me entiendo! ¡A veces!*
*Yo no soy mas duro para*
*decir a Diós: "¡Gracias, por*
*todo lo que Tu me das!" Pero,*
*gracias por mi amigo.*

## "HASN'T IT BEEN A LOVELY MORNING?"

### TUESDAY

Sardonic moans. . .overcoming sardonic feelings. . .weaving these lines into poems, into a poem. Spending days and days gazing. Reprimand me and castigate me; just don't obfuscate me. You're not Irish but you've got the "gift of gab." Don't ask him. He'd blow up and then you'd really have the "Bing Bang Theory!" Hysterical. He gets out of control. He rants: *"ru! ru! ru!"* Unwittingly, I found the solution for another character. You're not going to use that one on me, are you? That high tenor, fever. I cover my eyes and avoid him after imitating him. That shut him up. Can I ask a question?

### FRIDAY

He delivers his riddles with machine gun bullets. . .

### SATURDAY

The Papal Flax-Bearer went up in flames—*"sic transit"*—
formal invitations to pontifical ceremonies.

### THURSDAY

I pulled down my Venetian brows. Humor is healthy to an extent; like anything else, a good thing in measure; but it can lead to sardonic giggles.

### TUESDAY

Aren't you nauseated by this *plethora* of color? Don't let me try to impose my mortality on you. Fulminating sayings of wisdom, a nod to the odd. O.K., put it up! You'll get buried in your own perfection. Is that a syllogism or a parable?

## MYSTERIOUS FULMINATIONS

1.
I'm an anti-saint,
holy, but not according
to the canonical
categories, according
to the oddly composed
constitutions.

2.
I'll be buried with all my odd
ideas and the maggots
will take care of that.

3.
What to say?  You've heard it
all before, from a more original
sinner.


## HELD FOR RANSOM

Four years of youth,
seem fair progress,
from cheekiness,
to reticence.

For years from blush,
of innocence,
old age counts back,
in slow regress.

# THE COCKATIEL AND THE BOA CONSTRICTOR

1.

*Nymphicus hollanicus* is your Latin name, "quarrion," as you are known "down under," aviculturalists say you are non-aggressive, but why do you thrash with such violence against your cage bars? Budgies hold you in quick defeat; we humans, in feathery affection. They say you are perennial, of a sort: available year-round for the breeding and the buying. The child is tickled by you and the oldsome carry on with you as if some solemn philosopher. Color-words inadequately describe your varied splendor: albino, yellowish, pied, spotted, patched. *"Normal gray"* signs some special distinction. *"Sweet and gentle,"* they say. *"Tamable"* too. What do you do to us? Do we see in your glossy eyes our loneliness; in your clinging to your perch, your own timidity. Who can tame us, cockatiel?

2.

Neptune's priest, Lacoon, paid with sons his doom's due. Then he paid the sacrifice of life itself for suggesting the Truth. From Tenedos you came, in twins, hissing and churning in coiled fury, fire in your eyes and fire in your mouths, flailing the oceans with your armoured tails. " *Callidior cunctis animantibus agri,"* the Latin Fathers said of you. More cunning than any other beast in Paradise's sweet garden, you tickled the curiosity of demure Eve with your fast tongue and twisted modest Adam's love against her. Yet esoteric texts and orientalists tell us of your swelling slide from root *chakra* to fonatal. Some say you are fertility's and wellness's metaphor. But who can be sure? Cuddles and constrictions are known only by degree. Most think it best that you not be seen.

3.

Nature mitred you, making a hierophant's hat of feathers golden and slender: Aaron's pride, Zachary's heritage. You rise and bow in a solemn procession of emotions: a plume for fearlessness, a plea for preening, a tilt in that direction for some unseen frustration, a nod in this direction out of curiosity. With crested brilliance, you dominate your aviary. Familial to your feet, dimorphic to your beak, you tweek our feelings with the twitch of a rouged cheek. If pied, your behavior sexes you; your striped tail tells you are a lady, if light-colored. Do we socialize you or do you socialize us? Each shift in a keratin sheath signals a change, each thrash a storm unleashed and checked in a turn. Who knows the nature of your nightmares, who can tell the content of your ruffled dreams? Gesticulating mirror, shimmering echo to our sensibilities, you mock human sensitivity, laugh away our melancholy and time.

4.

Asklepios sits serene as you, snake, coil around his staff, this time bearing no hiss-heralded poison but balm of healing. Physicians and psychopomps, sacred and profane, wonder at you, intertwined with dreams in Elysian rites and counter-infections cures. Is it the kiss of *ephebos* or fang's lick drawing the toe's pain? In his marbled purifications, Apollo Belvedere does not shun you. Olgunius nightly embraces you. Faunus beckons to you from across the archetypal Tiber. *Coluber longissimus,* you braid your body around our sinews, tighten our tendons, incite our rage. You glide through our sexes and wing us from the *tholos* crypt of our ancestry to the palm branches of a still invisible Paradise.

# LINES ON LEARNING (PRINCIPLES AND PRACTICES CONCERNING CONTEMPLATIVE FORMATION: SECOND SERIES)

You feel that you are on the margin, standing on the fringe of all that is going on in the world.

\*

You don't much impress with your simple ways. Don't expect to.

Others love you in faulty ways, yet most with good intentions.

You meet others before you are ready. You are ready to meet others when you do not have to.

No multiplicity, no unity. No independence, no fusion. No differentiation, no non-differentiation.

Only when you are independent of others can you truly love them.

Rarely do you find the median line between disdain and over-affection.

You be what you want the other person to be. You do what you want the other person to do.

Learn the art of non-condemnatory judgement.

Share your readings, share your doings. Be to each other a source of constancy, in love and hope and living.

A hundred hurts will teach you resistance to remarks made for or against you. Be ever eager to meet the demands of a good word for others.

Be as hard shelled and slow as the Turtle. Be as supple and quick as the Lizard.

\*

Dare to articulate the questions others refuse to ponder.

Wage a relentless war on the rational.

Reduce things to their original simplification.

Let everything integrate itself.

Discover within what already is.

Truth reveals itself in time.

To discern the Spirit in a difficult situation, say only what is necessary to establish the Truth.

Truth is Truth, even in a glance.

For every statement made, a deeper silence pervades.

You can only do so many things. A fundamental choice determines all subsequent actions.

Enlarge your scenario.

When you play, you pray thrice.

Whether you exonerate or excoriate us, the degree of your own culpability is known to God alone.

Someone else's answers are stale bread on the table of Experience.

The transcendental moment is actually always there. You need not have the intensity of "feeling it" all the time.

The All and Everything is not here now.

*

Always speak your name like a question.

You do not have to save the World. That's done. Just take yourself less seriously. That is not.

We are all contemplatives: regretfully some refuse to admit it, more refuse to consider it, and most never think of it.

You magnify every decision into a metaphysical impossibility.

313

There is so much you know nothing about.

Don't strive for failure.

You put your hand to the plow and plowed a straight furrow. Unfortunately, the pasture is crooked.

You cannot examine an open wound with a needle. Let it heal!

When you lose your life, you lose it.

Were you speaking to us or only addressing your own ignorance?

A dose of your own sarcasm never hurts.

You are the object of your own subjectivity.

Avoid pretensions to the Throne of Truth.

Comatose? No, we just sleep in choir.

Your observership is our non-verbal evaluation. Your verbal evaluation of us is not desired.

God sits in the corner of the Cloister snickering at our self-imposed solemnity Laugh for God.

The humor in contemplative life is always serious. It is redemption from yourself.

Say your feeble *"Yes"* to God's soul-shattering call.

You have mastered the art of evasion. The realities have been denied their due. Now you hold court with delusion.

Depression is the flower of Beauty glowing in the cold night of life.

You feel hollow inside, but this time you are not empty.

We nail the Jesus in you to your cross.

Proficiency in what you do is the regeneration of a thousand failures.

Drink the dregs of loneliness. Greet the morning sun alone.

Fulfil your generative need by parenting the child within you, by healing the residual adolescent touchiness within you.

After the idols go, you seem to yourself a non-believer. When the false gods fall, you believe yourself to be an atheist.

Your director reigns as a benign despot.

*

You can't get your purpose from your teacher. Your teacher comes after your purpose.

# YOU STAY THE STUD ON THE STARCHED LINEN SHIRT

You stay the stud on the starched linen shirt of my memory, golden to the apples, corking to the clouds. You bore the beloved of your fancy and moss grass ecstasies, golden to the twigs which twitch to the touch. The heat of dreams, the sheets of chemistry rustling in the wind, the call of bones and alarm clocks hold you to the head board. She knows you another way, I know you thus, and shy and uncertain of the brass image in the looking glass looking straight back into your pounding chest. You guessed it was really you and you were never wrong, just alone. You walked the recalcitrance of your timbrous limbs yet prized them in the brawls of each evening. Insecurity carried you big like a truncheon before defeat, left you deflated after the explosions of the next to last conquest. Men mostly at war with themselves.

# EXXON STOP-OFF

EXXON stop-off:
memories of the
storm-tossed return,
glass and water,
gleam of emotions,
good will, no conflict,
age and youth in dialogue.

You were so much more
self-assured then. I was
not. Years tell truths we no
longer need to hide.

Friendship is
the name of regained
joy and strength.

# GOD DELIVER ME FROM THE RECENTLY REDEEMED

God deliver me from the recently redeemed.
They say I am not what I seemed.
I say they are not real enough for me:
sinner's force turns force for levelling everything
into a single equation, a simple denigration
of the human spirit into this or that, darkness
or light, sinner or saved.

God deliver me from the recently redeemed.
They trade their brain for a false security
called "faith." I say they believe in a God
of their own creation, a construction out of
need and wishful thinking, a desire for that
false acceptance called meeting the expectations
of others. Newly made saints are warriors of an
unequalled vengeance, ruthless in the scrutiny of me.

God deliver me from the recently redeemed.
They want to sell their bodies for a birthright
wrought of illusions, preconceptions of my personhood,
presuppositions of my necessities, rash judgements
of my deeds. Their desire is emotion over sentiment,
acquiescence above the pain of searching, smile to
entomb buried tears. They know better than I
myself this self's mission under grace.
God deliver me from the recently redeemed.

## MONKS AND MOURNING DOVES

The mourning doves are as
beautiful to me
as the chanting monks.

And the chanting
of the monks
is no less beautiful
for the mourning
of the doves.

Monks and mourning doves
are beautiful to me.


## YOU NEVER GAVE ME WHAT I WANTED

I wanted someone to talk to me.
You listened.

I wanted someone to hear me.
You responded.

I wanted help figuring it all out.
You understood me.

I wanted just plain tolerance.
You cared for me.

You never gave me what I wanted.
You gave me more than I can dream.

# REHEARSAL FOR LIFE

A line of groomsmen, a line of maids.
A family in transition, a moment in history.

There is a sympathy in the Universe. The half meets
the other half, the incomplete meets the other
incomplete, the unfinished meets the unfinished.

A line of groomsmen, a line of bride's maids.
A family in transition, a moment in history.

There is a harmony in the Universe. A dissonance
blends with a dissonance. The spark meets the
spark and the flame fills the darkness.

The Wedding Party, the fusion of hearts, desires,
aspirations, a hope for all good things, a harvest
time, a fullness.

A prayer. A Communion.


# THE MELDING OF MEN

Miniature volcanoes burn in the sand molds,
alloys flow like silver rivers,
air-hammers flatten sand like palms of Titans,
air-blowers and electronic buzzers batter the ears,
as John the Baptist turns forms upside down to
airbrush frequency. Silicone nightmares in the past.
Arms of industry loosen patterns air-hammered
all day long. Sandpit: Bentonite, pulverized clay
and bank sand. Northern sand from Lake Michigan and
Southern clay. Moisture. Water. Heat. Fire. Noise.
Poise. The perfection of team work.

# AIRBORNE:  FROM DAYTON TO ATLANTA

Flying through sunlight and clouds,
visibility obscured.
Mountain peaks of moisture.  Snow
sculptures of air and water.
Ear popping procedures once again.
Columns of clouds like phantoms.
A mirage of forms.
Chinese antiquities all in a row.
Polar bears.  Cotton candy pedestals.
Popcorn horizons.  Gladiators of foam and *Samurai.*
A haze of celestial Tabors and tall ships.
Puff-skyscrapers and plumes floating
below me and in the distance.

We possess none of it.
It belongs to none.

Parade balloons tethered to highways
and lakes shimmering below.
Table tops of whipped cream.
Dreadful *Hiroshima* along the skyscape.
My semi-queasy stomach floats
through the sky
in tired slow motion.
The deception of noise and altitude.
A sliver of silver and human flesh
cuts through the surroundings
of clean smoke.

Expectations were had for everyone
by everyone.

Water courses curve through the green
carpet below me.
Maple leaf patterns of sparkling water,
dross droppings of aluminum and
brass alloys.
Water works like silver bracelets.

Take a scoop of sky and clouds and
make of it a milkshake.
take life and make of it
dreams come true.

# COME HOME WITH ME

*"To cry to th' sea that roared to us. . ."*
    William Shakespeare, THE TEMPEST I.

1.

The troops advanced in phalanx formation,
helmeted ready with weapons arched,
weapons of war, weapons of the watch,
war youths, glory of their ancient nation,
steady youths, steady to their destination.

Two officers rode charioted to the vanguard,
brawny, tawny to the sun-bleached sky,
visors hard pressed against their piercing eyes,
winged Mars, arrowed Artemis, high on crest and sword,
steel hot soldiers bent to an eternal reward.

Close behind, a train of hoplites, forgemen, slaves,
waves of metal, waves of leather, waves of humanity,
dipped and rose, curved and bent to their destiny,
drummed march men, woodmen with their lathes,
mobile nation, noble, feckless to a thought of graves.

On they marched and on they went, on and on they rode,
weaponed to war and weaponed to their watch,
with shields and spears, swords and visors arched,
rock dust and gravel pressed against their load,
be it fair Fortune or Bane, relentless they strode.

So their thoughts, so their fancies, so the whimsy of the day,
so they rode and so their minds told of stories sacred
to their ears and to their hearts and memories protected,
sacred stories and protected memories their hearts relayed,
and those on wheels and those on foot in the silence prayed.

2.

Death slew them with Death's Indiscriminate Blade.
Down the helmeted, down in their phalanx form.
Down the youths, the steadfast youths, in their blood warm.

Down, down the visored officers against their chariots layed.
Down the hoplites, slain the workmen, cut down the slaves.

Slowly, slowly, then they came, a train of mourners sad,
waves of mortals, waves of women, waves of humanity,
dipped and cured, rose and bent to their destiny,
drummed mourners they marched atop the cracked swords,
atop weapons of war and watch crushed in dust's reward.

And on they marched and on they went their way,
mobile nation, savaged nobility, sobbing their sacred stories,
Persephone binding at their feet, Lethe poisoning their memories,
down the mortals, down the women, down humanity's way,
such the price and such the reward, so the whimsy of that day.

\*

This story we told to ourselves as we rode,
conscious as we were of our own moral imperative.
In my mind we were the two officers, Achilles and Patroclus,
which role we held I did not ask. There was power in the ambiguity,
there was mystery and magic in the uncertainty.

We knew we were in some unnamed way in the vanguard of
our own uncertainties. We wanted it that way.
It gave us power. It revealed mystery and magic as our own doing.
And so we rode and so we saw and so we told our secret
sacred stories to each other.

He could tell of fair Aphrodite blushing her
rounded form to the center of his manly palms,
hot to the mount and hot to the javelin of
her own forging. He was for me reluctant
Adonis, Achilles detected in his martial urge.

3.

Hermes, Hephaestus, Hector, Dionysius guided us and
chided us as we drove, knights on a flight
of fancy in open warfare with our shadows,
fighting our surreptitious selves for what was
real, combating the imbalance in each other.

Down the day and dark the night and dreadful
the edge of the cursing water. The dock boards
creaked as we sat, the weathered boards groaned.
Downward the pull, down, downward like the
fist of muscle that squeezes death from the groin
of man. Downward, downward the pull
of Death and Darkness like the muscle that
pulls all of life from the thigh of a man. Pain.
Pain the pleasure that drains life from the
bowels of man. Pain that pours green gold
oceans into the downward black throbbing
night of Black Water. Thick the ink of night
and thick the gravity-defying swirls of green
gold whirlpools sucking my mind downward
into the dark waters. Perverse the pleasure, more
perverse the desires, downward, downward into the
destruction of wanton selfishness. Kill Odysseus.
Murder meek-strong Penelope. Slay Telemachus if
you be Devil's Mentor. Evil the downward
pull of the life of a man, downward, out of
his thigh, and out of his groin, downward
out of his mind, suck his heart into the
downward throbbing Black Night Devil Waters.
Downward, downward, pulling yanking life
from the humanity of man. Pale, Neptune,
to the demonic destruction of Hero for Leander.
Down, down, sucked into the vacuum of an
eternity of selfish self-destruction. Horror the
horror wrecked on the House of Shame. Mind,
memory, heart, groin, pulled pitilessly into
an Eternal destruction of good. Horror the
churning black waters bouncing out of order,
coursing in Death's charade around each
footstep and heartbeat. Frozen the groin,
frozen the thigh, frozen the bronze torso in
the freezing wind.

4.

Frozen the heart and
frozen the mind in the freezing, burning

Waters, pulling me downward, downward to
the promised release of self-destruction.
Downward. Downward I was going. I wanted to
go down, from the weathered boards into the
churning Waters. I wanted to die there, thicker
in groin, and thigh, mind and heart, in the
swirling, burning, green gold waters, down, down,
into the destructive abyss of negative eternal
fusion with you and all who have caused me
pain by your very being. Down. Down, into
the black waters of Death's Desire for my soul.
I wanted that downward eternal ecstatic
spilling of my green gold self, my Black
Night self in Eternal release from the pain
I felt. I wanted it near you. I wanted it
there with you if I could not have it from
you. I wanted the weakness of my own
self-destruction. I wanted it more than the
strength of my own ordered desires.

*

Who of us knew who we were? Achilles and Patroclus.
Slaughtered were these heroes. Slaughtered all heroes
by the Fates, by jealous gods enraptured with
perishable mortals. Achilles, mowed down! Patroclus,
mowed down! Hector, mowed down! Shrewd Socrates,
mowed down! John the Baptist, mowed down!
And Jesus, mowed, mowed, down, down,
down the limits of his Divinity into our
Resurrection. Up! High on the Cross. High in the
sky, above us all. Nailed to the Universe of our
unending pain. Up! Upward! You called. No
touch, needless, no embrace. A Word. A
few words. Come! Come back! Come with
me! Come home with me, above the Hell
infested waters. Come home with me to Our
Mother and to our Brother and to Our Father.
Come! Come home with me.

5.

This story we lived with each other. We knew it.
We knew it in our minds and in our hearts. We
lived this story. We saw it with our own eyes and with
the eyes of each other. We felt the pain of the
necessary denial like a fist inside the chest,
near our hearts, about to pull them out.
My brother, my other knight, my hero, held
the greater pain. His heart had already been
ripped out by a Divine hand. My heart was
being ripped out by his. He loved me more than
I loved myself.

# I'VE DANCED WITH DEMONS

I've danced with
demons
through fiery tears,
wept with women
through their fears.

The eyes starved in the
seeing,
the hands left famished
through the touching,
the yearning coursing through
my being,
the satiety from nothing.

Exposing to everyone
my suppurating wounds,
an incomprehensible
object of loathing
and contempt.

Only the appearance of
innocence.


# SIGNS OF PROGRESS IN THE SPIRITUAL LIFE

Now, when I stand me
up to speak,
I pray the
Lord to keep me weak.

And should I awake
before I die.
I'll thank the Lord
I learned to cry.

# MY CHANGED FRIEND

The slipping of the sunlight from the road's edge,
the pulling of moonlight from the yard's hedge,
the spilling of the cascading waters over the ledge,
the last echo of the words after we spoke our pledge,
it carves a hollow through my heaving chest:  your death.

The tapping of the dawn on my window sill,
the moon bounding down this to that and every hill,
the flowing tides measured out with the greatest skill,
the baby's first-time laughter giving parents a thrill,
it grows like love's warmth in my heart:  your memory.


# SAINT JOHN OF *ASCESIS*

Saint John of *Ascesis*
pray for us.
Saint John of *Ascesis,*
save us from ourselves.
Saint John of *Ascesis,*
your laughter is a
salve for us. . .
in sorrow,
rejection,
false hope.
Saint John of *Ascesis,*
pray!

## EAT YOUR HEART, *SUN TZU!*

After the manner of THE ART OF WAR.

I bruised my heart with barbed wire
looking for an escape from you.

I antagonized the giants
looking for a twin soul like me.

I tore the shirrings of my mind
trying to rip myself free from memories.

I regarded my equals with compassion
and they harassed me.

I had too delicate a sense of honor
and my inferiors calumniated me.

I was too quick of temper
and my elders made me into a fool.

I was cowardly
and my shadow-self caught me.

At last, I was reckless,
and life itself killed me.


## THE SKULL

The skull on the
desk in my cell
is mine.

# CATHEDRAL DOORS:  DOORS TO THE HEART

*"Knock and it shall be opened unto you."*  MATTHEW 7:7

Cologne Cathedral:
knocking at its
great doors,
persistently,
only suddenly,
to find yourself
within,
let in by Jesus.
Knock enough
and you shall find
yourself, your
true self
with Him:  This is the
integrity of truth
and work and order.


# MEDITATION ON AN ICON OF OUR LADY OF *KYKKOS*

Our Lady of *Kykkos*
by *Simon Ashakov* 1668
Moscow, *Tretyakov* Gallery

\*

The mystery of Motherhood
and Sonhood and Birthship
and Growth.
The Full Man:  Christ,
first as Baby in human arms.
How we struggle to love
and to be free!
How to imitate Him
in loving and in Freedom?

The Mystery: to somehow
reconcile the tension between
the begetting and the parting
and the coming and the letting
go.


## MY OWN ROSE

My old Rose grows lovelier sure
than I in ways and deeds,
her hours, for others, cast in prayer,
her words, to each, a life-seed.
My worn Rose glows holier true
than I am of grace just now,
gentler she is, her thoughts like dew,
shimmering across her brow.
My torn Rose wins higher nobility
that I, with power, cannot show,
thorny pains she bears in simplicity,
red-petalled her mystic crown.
    Tinctured bright, to her souls' pitch delicate;
    My own Rose: perennially Love's dedicate.

# THE HARVESTING OF THE DEER

*"Therefore I will shake the heavens, and the earth shall remove out of her place, in the wrath of the Lord of hosts, and in the day of his fierce anger. And it shall be as the chased roe, and as a sheep that no man taketh up: they shall every man turn to his own people, and flee every one into his own land. Every one that is found shall be thrust through; and every one that is joined unto them shall fall by the sword."* ISIAH 13:13 (KJV)

I.

Environment, habitat, the rabbit in the honeysuckle, quail,
the box elder, all tell you what condition we are in.
I am a year and a half old buck. There is a doe on the
home-range here. We know our boundaries, our harvest
pressure, the denser areas, the South River and Honey
Creek. We know the tailoring they call, *"the harvesting of
the deer."*

The old roe is at once the most alert. She knows the land
and the resources. She sees the big antlers and the firearms.
She knows the hunters' "rights." We all browse through the
honeysuckle and the goldenrod. We know the winged and
the scarlet sumac, we know the hidden passageways of the
hedge rows, our private retreats.

Wildlife, habitat, we all leave our trailings, even the bluebird
on the property. Edges, hedges, cover. The place,
says the Poet is a *"state of mind."* We have no mind to own
it for ourselves. We find ourselves "here" and make the best
of what is given. Turkeys, wood ducks, fowls of all species,
mass crop failures. . . the acorns are scarce
this year. I marvel at the beams of the roebuck's antlers as
the glancing sun graces him a premonition
of the gun that might blow him from us. Pine tops, natural
food sources, impeding growth, impending death.

Lean deer forage, eat acorns by the pound, hulls too.
We like soft, moist clover, we eat soft *tofu,* oriental oak,
native persimmons, most any crop, mineral powders, rye,
top soil fills of elements and insects. We see povets
picking seeds.

Cedar fields and pine groves along the clay currents,
fallow, spurts of young growth. There are the free-ranging
predators who rob us of our fill, nesting ones, dogs,
resident species slinking in the hard woods, white oaks.
They leave me moot.

II.

*"For the benefit of the wildlife,"* they come. Bow hunters,
proficient with their chosen devices. Foxes?
Where did you see falcons? No, decisions are not made
in a vacuum. One man's sport is another's destruction.
*Kudzu* kills. Frost destroys. One is displaced, the other
comes from Nature, beyond our control. One deer and one
hunter is one reflection of all that is going on in the woods.
*"The harvesting of the deer,"* they call it, a change in our
ecology to produce foraging and better growth.

Coastal Bermuda, rye grass, woody stems; we browse, nip
at twigs, enjoy it all. We bucks love the thickets.
They are our Conyers Mall. We gather, frisk, run, play,
bond, "raise hell," delight in being young. Then we hide.
We hear traffic across the waters and the pavements. We
shift our patterns in our fright. We move about and
we move around from the first crack of dawn over the jagged
horizon until the last glimmer of light has gone.

Then arrives our nocturnal nesting. Who says we bucks
come from nowhere, have no sensations, are not given to
the "feelings of the heart?" Fawns, does, bucks, babies,
mothers, fathers, families, friendships, courtships
across the glistening meadowlands. The doe conceives.
The fawn is born. We're spotted, and dappled, and
burnished and bristling from the tips of our tails to the
pinnacles of our points. We drop and spurt and slip
and skip and skirt the parameters all around us
in a cacophony of color and movement. We are
serene and we are tenacious.

III.

The *"quality of the hunt,"* the bowmen say, has something
to do with the quality of the light and the quality of the
movement in all of Nature. Hunters are serene and

tenacious too, claiming a conservative ethic. The centers
of their eyes are high-voltage coronas in electric,
magnetic radiation. They control the burning and the
humidity which surrounds us. They ferret us out,
they burn needles in the pine stands, shatter sweet gums
with timber for outposts, defy night light with infrared rays,
wear commando clothes to deceive us. They whistle with
the togies and the songbirds. Seedlings resprout as
redoubts, pulpwood parapets, a new militarism, a genetic
rearrangement within the Cosmos, war games fought with
ancient archetypes on Sunday afternoons.

IV.
The gray grasshopper, the green-gray preying mantis.
The groundhog and the starlings. Longbow and compound
bows. Fletchers fingering feathers in the breeze. 40 lb.
pulls minimum. Crossbows, arrows latched in for quick
release. Somewhere hidden: Beretta and Brownings.
Remingtons somewhere left on their mahogany truck racks.

Attitudes poised to action. Details trimmed to the kill.
The desired display of the "harvested" game. The trophy
toted home at the end of the day. Tarps spread on the
flatbed of the pickups. The dangling, banging of the head
against the tailgate. Image: from the bootlaces up to the
face paint, the influence of the drug, the chemical in the
throbbing vein, the residue of the alcohol on fetid breath.

V.
I mutter to myself, *"Avoid pitfall. Deadfall. Snare. Steer
clear of steel, catch, trap, net. Salt licks have the lick of
death. Flee live decoys. Don't chomp on carrion. They
have baited hooks. Listen for unnatural sounds. Electric
sizzles, seeps of gas, hiss of fire from kerosene.*

*Tilt antlers. Clean hide. Don't wag tail. Lay low like
squirrels. Movement has the look of death. Keep sight.
Don't be blinded by car lights."*

Then metal click; automatic pistols. Glare of axe shimmer
of cleats. The whelp of dogs. Then flash of 500 square
inches of daylight, fluorescent orange above waistline.

VI.

*"Processed for consumption,"* they advertise it.  Transported
from the field.  *"Field dressed,"* they call our gutting.  Cut up,
wrapped up, and frozen.

"Field dressed deer" indeed:  all our organs in our chests
and intestinal cavities removed.  Autopsies at our death site.

Tree-stands.  Climbing.  Non-climbing.  Concealed.
Aluminum and seed do not grow from the earth here.
They are invaders, invaders in our habitat.

Intact, unmodified, and unmounted antlers and skull-plate,
natural air drying.  The grunt of the mallard drake.  The
scream of the deer.

Coues, white tails, black tails.  Camouflage conceals, blends
with natural surroundings, breaks up the "human outline."
Trees.  Limbs.  Open spaces.  Faces.  Branches.  Shanks.
Patches of sky.  Thighs.  Holes in the pattern.  Holes in the
deer.

VII.

Raccoons.  Opossums.  Rabbits.  Doves.  Crows.
Scavenger birds.  Owls.  Battery-powered lights
(n. ex. 6 volts).  Fuel lanterns.  30 minutes after sunset—
30 minutes before sunrise.  Unlawful hours.  Periods of
reprieve.  Still hunting:  no dogs.  Death slinks like Silence
in the twilight.  The "tagging of the carcass" on the site
of the kill.  Legalities:  *"Fill out properly."*  *"Leave on deer"*
until *"Processed for consumption."*  Human laws do not
protect us from human crimes.

VIII.

I long for waters cool and running,
waters warm and humming to my soul.
I thirst for rivulets wet and clear,
springs, falls, rivers to my refreshment flowing.

I yearn for a liquid to quench my thirst,
a liquid beyond taste and sight, a light
slowly welling up to fill my hungry being,
a welling of redemption over my mortal nature cursed.

My nourishment is my straining higher,
my nurturement is my pining from deep below,
running, coursing, flowing, welling, wide within
with a swelling of my soul in this spiritual fire.

IX.
My tormentors torture me, my fathomless fears:
where is the pavilion of lasting peace, rest?
Where is the feast of sweet repose from the
hunt, from the relentless pursuit, from my tears?

X.
I am a buck of ample strength for my youth,
I am a runt of steady glide and ready grace,
I am as ruddy as the earth, glorious as the sun,
I am a feast to my eyes and this is my truth.

XI.
Why do I sigh within me?  Where is my hope?
All of my kind carry a death-script written
in our sinews and in our bones, centered it is
to our very marrow.  Death peers through a bow scope.

Why so downcast?  Why this constant dejection?
Our pride is our tribe.  Our herd is our fame.
My name is written in wonder and ancient poetry.
The turn of the Wheel is not my personal rejection.

XII.
From the pine peaks through hard woods I leap.
From the craggy rocks to the clay paths I run.
From the dogwoods to the swamp's edge I prance.
From the bottom lands to the ridge tops my jump is steep.

Deep, deep, deep within I hear the roaring of the ages.
The roaring is deep in my hooves and deep in my
calves.  It tumbles through my tendons and travels
through my arteries to my brain where it always rages.

XIII.
The roaring humbles me, the roaring frightens me.
It is the pulse of finitude, it is the enduring
of all things without me.  It is the movement of
Eternity.  It is the unwinding of my destiny.

XIV.
I long for a silence beyond the gurgling waters.
I hunger for a fulfillment beyond my foraged food.
I stretch to an expectation without given proof.
I strain for that immortality no creature can author.

XV.
There is a treachery and cunning in the givenness of things.
There is an oppression from once never-imaged enemies.
There is an abandonment in the very getting of life.
There is the coming of the end when the night owl sings.

EPILOGUE:

Scrape of the blade in the cutting of the belly.  Scrape of the
blade in the cutting of the mouth.  One back tooth ground down,
one year old buck.  *"He is small."*

Hunter One: *"He shit on me."*  Deer Processor One: *"Shot
me, I'd probably shit on you too."*

Sawing of the sinews and bones.  The blood on the fingers.
The spraying with the hose in the hollow of the carcass.
The pouring of the fluids.  Blood clots under the boots.
The piercing of the back tendons through the fur.  *"A buck
whose points have not broken through is called a 'Button
Buck.'  His horns haven't broken before he has been slain."*

The cutting of the testicles, split right down the middle.
Strung up on steel.  The drawl of the speakers.  The silence
of the deer.  *"Let them hang for three days."*  The yellow and
the red and blue plastic bins in the cooler, filled with guts,
hooves, fur, pelts, flat on the iron gridiron.  Items for the
cosmetic industry.

The rancid smell that permeates the clothes, the hair, the skin, the poet's folio, leaves, as much as the poet's ink. The glaze in the eye, the guts in the hand. The front hooves in the air. The tail on the wall. The gore in the hands. The cleanness of the cuts. The resistance of the bond structures. The place, says the Poet, is a *"state of mind."*

The jab of the blade, the gurgle of the blood from the first gash, the second thrust, the pulling of the halves to their flat hemispheres. The distortion in the brain, the discrimination of the feelings. *"And it shall be as the chased roe. . ."*

ANDALUSIA:  FOR MARY FLANNERY
O'CONNOR (1925—1964)

*". . . for the fashion of this world passeth away."*

I CORINTHIANS 7:31

On the chipped brick steps of your Andalusia Home,
I stand alone.  Equinox, son of Ernest and Marquita,
and Flossie, blond cross-bred hinney of another lineage,
somewhere feed, unsuspecting *ikons* for an
international symposium keepsake T-shirt.

A black cat arrives, stares hard, approaches warily and
whines at me. " *Hello, Flannery!  Green-eyed Flannery
in your feline incarnation, Jasmin!*" TWO,
missing for five days I'm told, nowhere to be seen,
is really "Primo."

From the limb-jammed front pasture pond, I view
your farm.  Natural light illumines the upper window over
your writing room, catches off your crutch's metal
as you stoop to wave.  Creatures and critters cry for you
to the crush of cars up and down Highway 441.

I love the solitude of your supernatural spaces.
A Japanese iris, single, tall, crimson, rises straight up from
a cloister of green leaves, right into the air like a flare
of sanctifying grace, emblem of you in glory and power,
sentinel now to my silent regret.

This soft yellow Georgia sun, peeking above your second
floor roof, is an image of your passing beauty.  Gracious
to the last, yes, it is you, so quick to disappear when the
mannered presence is no longer needed.  How much
the South has changed since your departure!

I now lose myself in the gnarl of woods and thoughts and
brown weathered boards.  Trundling through the tangle
of this wild grass and these tender emotions, my heart
hurts to serve you.  A dangling branch stick figure, in the
white light of your sun, struts from "Caution" to "Go."

Now, here, in this long forsaken field, an immense white flag
is flung to the sky.  Snorts swell through the pines.  A hind
rushes to buried waters.  You, Flannery, dance through the
decay of clay and lupus needles, consecrated in your
longing for things beyond human form.

Your fingers whisk along the lines of my ruled note paper.
A red glaze comes to the tree trunks in furnace heat.
Yours is the glow on these baked black-wire boundaries
to my path of necessary return.  Yours is the precious
peace, the cool breeze of momentary serenity in my brain.

Mystery you demanded and Mystery you provide.  The
blue heron flutters like a fictive cripple in my phantasms.
Thomistic to the toes, your funny bone is the bent spine
holding all principles to human task.  Your voice rings out:
*"IT IS HUMAN TO FALL.  NO FALL, NO REDEMPTION!"*

A crinkling, massive evergreen here rises, stupefying as a
peacock, over your lonesome white clap-board home, ready
to wriggle in all its blazing green and bronze brilliance,
cones like eyes, eyes like scalpels puncturing my
possessiveness.  The sniff of ecstasy fades and I am gone.

## POE'S PUB

The boogie on the radio.
The beer on tap.  The ice
floating in the glasses of tea
and Coca Cola.  Talk of everything
from chimneys, conversion,
Catholicism.


## FOR THE RETREAT MASTER

Fore the sore seat—no thanks.
For the provocation—I'm not sure.
For the erudition—my admiration.
For the retreat—my gratitude.


## A CHILD'S RIDDLE

If I were Tyler
and you were Dad
I'd be glad.
If I was bad
and you were mad
I'd be sad.
Would you hold me still
like you do
when I get ill?
Will my dreams come true?
Will you always be you
and always love me
through and through?

# WHY NOT YOU?

They say
third needs
to be different
especially if
gender repeat
and
if not
worst of all three
then best
of one
and two.

Why
not
you?


# FLIGHT 215 FOR ST. PETERSBURG, FLORIDA

*"He covered them with a cloud."*

PSALM 105:39

Glorious, glorious clouds,
Ear popping clouds.
Brilliant snow white clouds,
luminous on my yellow pad.
Blinding clouds.
Westward sun on
my right.

# AIRBORNE OVER FLORIDA

*"And God said, 'Let there be a firmament in the midst of the waters, and let it divide the waters from the waters.'"*     GENESIS 1:6

The vast ganglia of tributaries
of the coastline, islands, then water,
water, water. Specks of boats and ships
indented in the ripples. Edges of water
and dimensions of water. And textures
of water. And fringes of water in the
glistening sunlight. Pockets of water
and pools of water within the shifting
waters. Veins of water and conduits
of water. And water of ice in my
plastic cup. Blue water and steel gray
water and silver water and gold water.
All against an azure sky.

The waters of Baptism, of John
and Jesus and Flannery O'Connor's
"The River." Cleansing waters,
soothing waters, healing waters.

The whirl of the down-speeding
of the jet. Sandbars. Pressure
build-up in the ears.

Water like leather and water like
warm skin. Ships like planes
with white tails behind.

I have no need to plunge into the
healing or life-defying waters. The
waters have already come to me.
This flight is a Confirmation.

# PALMS OF PASADENA HOSPITAL #1

11:00 P.M.  Palms of Pasadena Hospital.
Visiting with my Father, Mother and
Sisters.  The pain of a protracted
discernment.  Death is not imminent,
only anxiety.  The inability to make
decisions.  The fear of letting go.

\*

Trying to maintain a course
steady into reality but it is not easy
because of so many perspective and
attitudinal shifts.  Compassion must be
primary.

\*

Alone with my Father for a while.
The preoccupation of TV.  But there is the
peace and quiet of being together.

\*

DNR
No respirator.
No artificial means.
4 liters of oxygen?
Vasotec—reduces the afterload.

\*

My Father, all of us,
are tired from the activities of the
day.  The view, earlier, of *Boca*
Ciega Bay was uplifting.  Visits with
friends help balance
perspectives and emotions.  We are
all being stretched into new life.

# EVENING RIDE HOME FROM THE HOSPITAL

Full red sun
over the Gulf
peering through the Grenadine
palms


# 6342 18TH AVENUE NORTH:
# MORNING

6:40 A.M.  The cool air of
this early hour and the birds and
cars in their incoherent choruses start
me off.  I live in the reality of the
moment, with the nag of the
mosquitos at my ear and legs.  The
lizards must be dormant.  Perhaps
I make too much of everything and
not enough of somethings.  *"Just life!"*
And just one person's solitary life being
lived out in conjunction with others,
family, friends, the intimacy of the
professional caregivers, mostly strangers.
And the recurrent themes of PSALM 139:10.
*"If I take the winds of the dawn, if
I settle at the farthest limits of the sea,
Even then your hand shall guide me,
and your right hand hold me fast."*
The light rain has passed, after
dropping in my tea and on my Bible
pages.

# TREASURE ISLAND BEACH

A solitary pelican passes, as I stand
in the shell-textured sand, the Gulf's
warm waves wrapping around my legs
and thighs.  I love the roar of the water,
the patterns in the dark clouds, left, and
the white clouds, right.  Bilmar Hotel
nearby.  This is a return to my mystical
experiences of February, 1992:  *"If I take
the wings of the dawn, if I settle at
the farthest limits of the sea.  Even
then your hand shall guide me, and
your right hand hold me fast."* ( PSALM 139:
9-10.)

It was wonderful!  I went for the
plunge and got completely soaked
in the warm gritty waves.
Warm, wet, gritty Gulf water,
dripping down my chest and thighs,
legs tingling in the cross-breeze.
The smell of life and decay, seagulls
pecking through the shells for food.
A glider-kite hovers on the horizon, right.
There is life, new life in a single shift
of perspective, a change of view.  And
always, new sounds.

I watch the slow passage of the
shell collectors, their plastic bags and
shoulder pouches near to hand.
The clouds break to greater clarity.
There is a turning in me of mood.
The "Baptismal Waters" have cleansed
me.  I am connected to all.

A young family passes us.  The
beach population grows and my sister
approaches.

I love to see my flat-foot
impressions in the sand. I gather
the tassels of *pampas* grass from a
mound. The warm breeze cools me off
as I dry. And my sister speaks
to me of the passing of our family
from this place and our visions for the
future. Seagulls squawk and chirp
in expectation of something.


## TREASURE ISLAND PLAZA

Waiting as our laundry dries. I've been able to situate myself
with the help of some store clerks, a map and some postcards. Also, some
remembered parameters. What keeps coming to me is this basic, central theme:
Life! All ages, men, women, various couplings. Life, opportunities, growth,
change.


## I DELIGHT

I delight
in the flight
of the pelican.

## TREASURE ISLAND COMMUNITY CENTER AND PARK

The
thud
of
a beach
ball
and
the
shrill
tones
of
the
children
playing
. . .


## THE GREEN LIZARD

The green lizard swells its peach-tongued
throat, languid on the log below the
deck.  I have sea creatures all over me;
shells and flotsam and jetsam.

# PALMS OF PASADENA HOSPITAL #2

Room 366.  A quiet visit with my Dad.
The lovely cloud formations.  And with the
clouds we watch the drifting of our
past days into a new tomorrow.  The
course is as natural as Nature gives
of herself, but the specifics and the
parameters are personal.

\*

We are in a protracted death watch now.
All travel plans have been dropped
and flights must be canceled.  My Father
will die here in Florida.  My Mother is resigned
to the situation.  We've had our words of love
and plenty of silent prayer.  I watch the
waning of power.  *"Not to us, O Lord,
not to us."*  (PSALM 115:1.)

*"Only a breath are mortal men; an illusion
are men of rank.  In a balance they prove
lighter, all together, than a breath."*
(PSALM 62:10.)

\*

I sit here alone with my Father.  There is
peace and resolution in the situation.
And a full silence.

\*

A kite over Boca Ciega Bay lifts my spirits.
Soft white clouds puff through blue sky.
We go from what seems to be a death watch
to watching my Father get stronger.
A weariness.

# NATURE SOOTHES ME

A snake slithers along the walk.
Now I see lizards climb vertically
up the outside walls of the house.
The sun on my skin heats me up and
my sweat cools me off.
Nature soothes me.  *"Let everything
that has breath, praise the Lord!
Alleluia."*  (PSALM 150:6.)

## *BOCA CIEGA BAY*

I'm sitting on a wooden bench on
a wooden deck stretched out into Boca
Ciega Bay, with the Bridge 80° ahead
to my right, and the Habitat.  I love
the harmony of the speed boats, the lapping
water, the cars, the planes, the wind chimes.

A snow white seagull flaps and hovers
and chirps over my head.  The sun, west,
designs a pyramid of wet shards
directly to my side.  I shade my eyes
and feel cooler immediately.

There is the ebb and flow of my Father's
strength and of his mental clarity.  I wish
he could enjoy this natural and man-made
serenity so close to his hospital room.

A pelican prances in the muck at the base
of the bridge near survey marker 0+6.
The reek fills my nostrils.  A fish pops up
as I skip a shell back into the Bay.

# PALMS OF PASADENA HOSPITAL #3

Hospital meditation chapel.  A
prayer book, three kneelers and
an altar with a crucifix, a plain
cross and the TORAH inside a
Star of David.  Three bibles.  Literature
on healing and pastoral care.  A
quiet moment, a simple prayer:
*"O Lord, help us resolve our situation."*

*

Overcast sky outside our window.

*

Trying to explain to my Father
the exigencies of his situation.

*

The conversation turns to the
gimmicks and gadgets of Delani Street
and the live Nativity Scene at Radio
City in New York.  Various family holidays.
Chinatown and the animals and smells of
Puerto Rico.

*

Across the hall I see through the windows
a sky of blue laced with gray and white clouds.
Now here in room 366 the window reveals
a cloud shrouded sun.

*

I sit in the Admissions section
of the Emergency unit, waiting for my
family.  Many details and specifics have
been looked at today.  We have much

to face in the days ahead.  We are all
learners and active participants in this
family crisis.  Real-life traumas here in this
room and TV reproductions of Florida
State Trooper arrests.  Florida reality.
Causes for prayer.


## PALMS OF PASADENA HOSPITAL #4

NOTES:

2:54 A.M.  Difficulties/acceleration.

2:55 A.M.  Not breathing.

No great change.  Heart stopped
functioning on its own.

Organ donation?  Yes.

National Cremation Society.

My Father passed away at
2:55 A.M. here from problems
related to his heart.

# THE RAIN CONTINUES ITS STEADY FALL

3:48 P.M.  I am here at the West Entrance
to Montgomery Ward Department Store across
Tyrone Blvd., not far from the
house where we are staying.  The rain
continues its steady fall, as it has these
past two hours I have been away.

I've needed the solitude and the
walking and the rain.  I've needed
this time alone with my Father, away
from my family.  I have felt the
ebbing of the power and the inflowing
of the tenderness.

I last saw my Father as a loveable, little,
old, helpless man fighting a good
fight for everyone else's sake.  He
was tired and ready to go and I
have the blessing of being the last
family member to see him alive,
like a child, like Brother Mark
Crow, his frightened eyes, his
confusion, his face being smoothed
by lotion gently applied by
his nurse.

We had our peace-filled words, our
hug and kiss and gesture goodbye.
It's not a blur, it's a still
frame, my last image of him in
his chair, strapped for protection,
with oxygen and intravenous tube.

And then this morning, the cadaver,
the supple limbs of an old man
asleep with his mouth open, hair
mussed.  The shell of power, the
husk of new life.  *"Seventy is
the sum of our years, eighty if we
are strong."* (PSALM 90:10.).  He was 76.

I loved him with a gentle love in the
*persona* of his transformation these
past few days. We had our time
alone, our time to speak together
and our time to be silent together.

There was the laughter and the
agitation of his confinement. Once,
when he removed his oxygen, he
exclaimed: *"I want freedom!"*
It was an exclamation I could laud and
did deep in my soul. And now
he has it.

# CODA:

# A YOUNG MAN'S DREAM, AN OLDER MAN'S VISION

The wood of the polished desk, once used by a monk, shimmers like silk fabric, clear, over a leather writing case. Movement in the mind signals movement in the flesh as well, and back and forth. We cannot capture our boyhood fantasies. They only sometimes return to chagrin us in our lost idealism. I recall the strength of my lost Father like the early infatuations of my lost youth. Regrets. Where am I headed? Is it into further misery? Not if I choose otherwise. Old men dream dreams of a recaptured past. Young men see visions without discouragement, not knowing the disillusionment to come. Youth knows of heroics. Old men know the war wounds. The young man smiles to me from the photograph, my eye an unsuspected lens when that lens caught him in a bright moment in his life, his loved one under the shelter of his left shoulder. What does life demand of us who have never been there?